AF261448

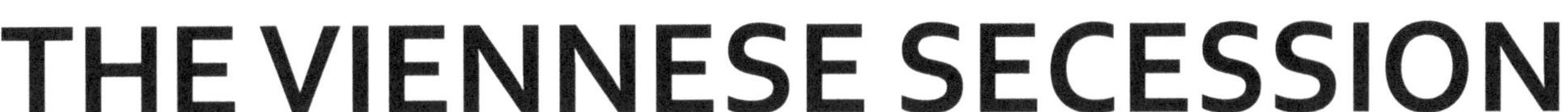

THE VIENNESE SECESSION

Author: Klaus H. Carl and Victoria Charles

Layout:
Baseline Co. Ltd,
District 3, Ho Chi Minh City
Vietnam

ISBN: 978-1-68325-941-1

Printed in

Klaus H. Carl & Victoria Charles

THE VIENNESE SECESSION

Klimt, Schiele, and the art of modern Vienna

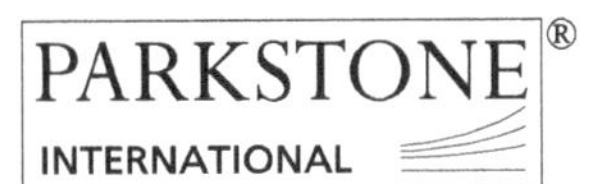

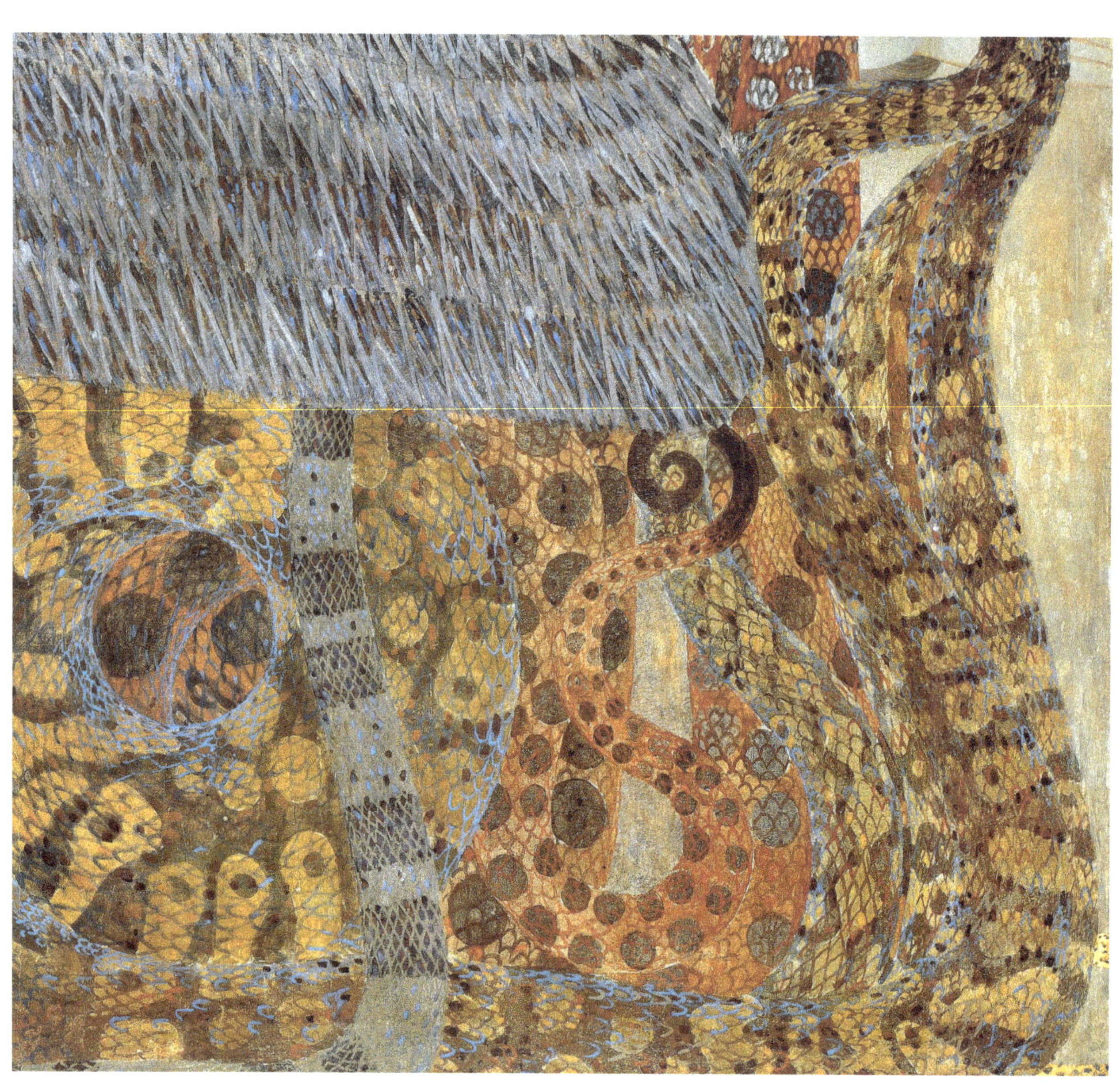

CONTENTS

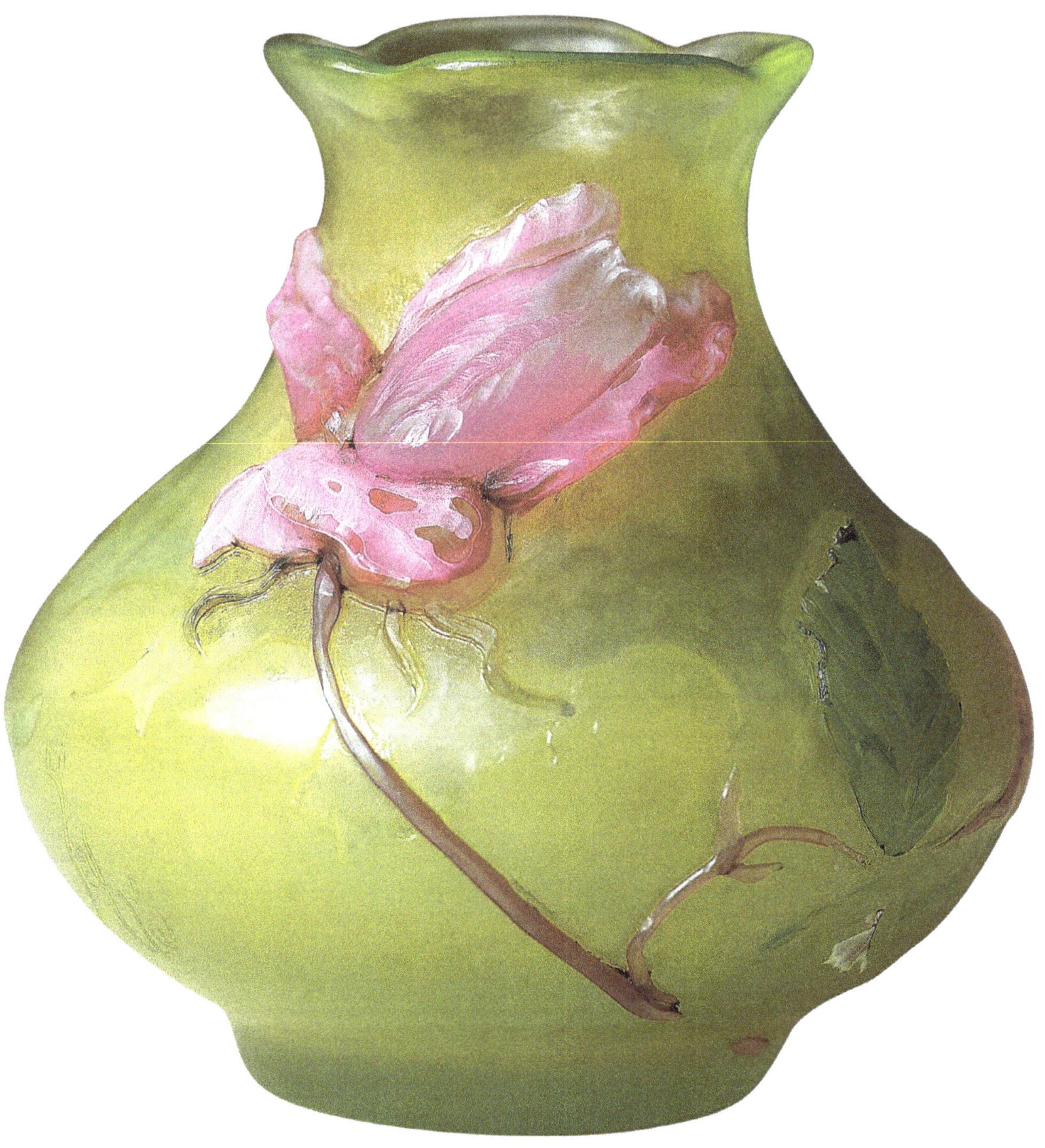

INTRODUCTION

ven though the Viennese upper class were passionately fond of dances, the opera, theatre, and music, they remained extremely conservative. Strict Catholicism accompanied by rigid social morals made them seem, at least in appearance, unmoving and close-lipped. While the rest of society was only too happy to embrace all sorts of pleasures then deemed sensual, for example the waltz, the so-called "good" society rejected any topic that was unaesthetic, erotic or even mildly sexual. Thus different standards were applied to different strata of society, which is telling about the dominant concept of morality in Vienna in particular, and the Austro-Hungarian Empire in general, at the end of the 19th century.

In these decades, Vienna was a city at the zenith of its power and influence. Kaiser Franz Joseph I was the monarch of an empire of over fifty million people, encompassing several dozen constituent kingdoms and duchies from Bohemia to Serbia. However, at the end of World War I, at the beginning of 1918, the empire only had several months of existence left. With Kaiser Karl's failed attempt to conserve the empire in the form of a federal state, Austria suddenly became a small nation of seven million inhabitants, of which three million lived in and around Vienna. Barely twenty years later, Nazi Germany under Adolf Hitler would annex the Republic, thus sealing its fate in the tumultuous years to follow.

However, the decline of Austria had begun long before the events of 1918 or 1934. Successions of military defeats were already a clear warning sign that the prolonged existence of the empire was not guaranteed. Furthermore, the rising impoverishment of thousands of Czechs, Hungarians, Poles, Jews, Romanians, and Romani led many to leave the poorest parts of the empire to look for work in the capital. But their lot did not improve as the city could not provide enough work and accommodation, which led them to live in worse conditions than before. These social problems were ignored by the rich and influential citizens of Vienna who decided to blind and distract themselves with a true flurry of pleasure-filled activities instead.

▲ **Gustav Klimt,**
Gnawing Sorrow (detail from second panel *of The Beethoven Frieze),* 19
Casein on plaster, height: 220 cm.
Secession, Vienna.

◀ **Émile Gallé,**
Orchid Vase.
Glass with inserted ornaments and relief.
Private collection.

These developments also influenced the decorative arts, which witnessed a lot of change and upheaval between the decline of the influential French style and the World Fair in Paris in 1889, which was held in honour of the hundredth birthday of the French Revolution. There was no simple and fluid transition from one style to another. Between the rise of new ideas and artistic techniques, older styles were consistently resurrected. Even as late as 1900, artistic influences popularised during the time of the European Restoration, or French art during the reign of Napoleon III, could still be seen in the exhibits of the World Fair. Nevertheless, the imitation of these styles was not consistent enough for a coherent movement to form, mainly because there were many artists who wanted to distinguish themselves from their predecessors by expressing their own decorative ideals.

Despite their novelty, these new movements were not isolated from the influences of their predecessors. They were characterised by weariness from seeing the old forms and patterns repeated over and over again, from having to face the infinite imitation of furniture from the time of the French kings that all answered to the name of "Louis", beginning with Louis XIII (1601-1643), followed by Louis XIV (1643-1715) to Louis XVI (1754–1793). They were also characterised by a general dismissal of the common shapes and pattern of the Gothic style and the Renaissance. In essence, this new movement stood for the acceptance of a new art that was grounded in the modern age and not dependent on previous influences for credibility.

Before 1789, the year that marked the end of the *Ancien Régime*, different styles usually developed with dependence on the monarchs; this new

century wanted its own style. The desire for freedom from art and fashion dictated by rulers and sovereigns was not only perceivable in France but also beyond its borders. Many countries in Europe witnessed the slow awakening of proud nationalism that was rooted in the wish for literature and art that could be called their own. In short, this desire created the emergence of new understanding and appreciation of art that was not a servile copy of past glory and even less an imitation of foreign influences. In addition, contrary to previous decades, the need for applied art skyrocketed, mainly because this branch of art had nearly died out in the 19th century. In the past, everything was richly decorated: from home décor and dresses to weapons and simple household objects. Every object possessed its own ornaments and its own beauty and elegance. The 19th century, on the other hand, essentially looked for functionality rather than elegance. Beauty, elegance and ornaments became superfluous. This century, which began with a totalitarian indifference towards decorative beauty and elegance, ended so sadly in the brutal disregard of international human rights, was characterised by a paralysis of taste and aesthetics.

The return of the exiled concept of aesthetics was also at the heart of the Art Nouveau movement and its Austro-German manifestation, the *Jugendstil*. In France, people began to feel the absurdity of the situation and started to demand creativity, innovation and authenticity from cabinetmakers, decorators, stucco specialists, and even architects. This gave rise to a form of applied art that directly catered to the need of a new generation.

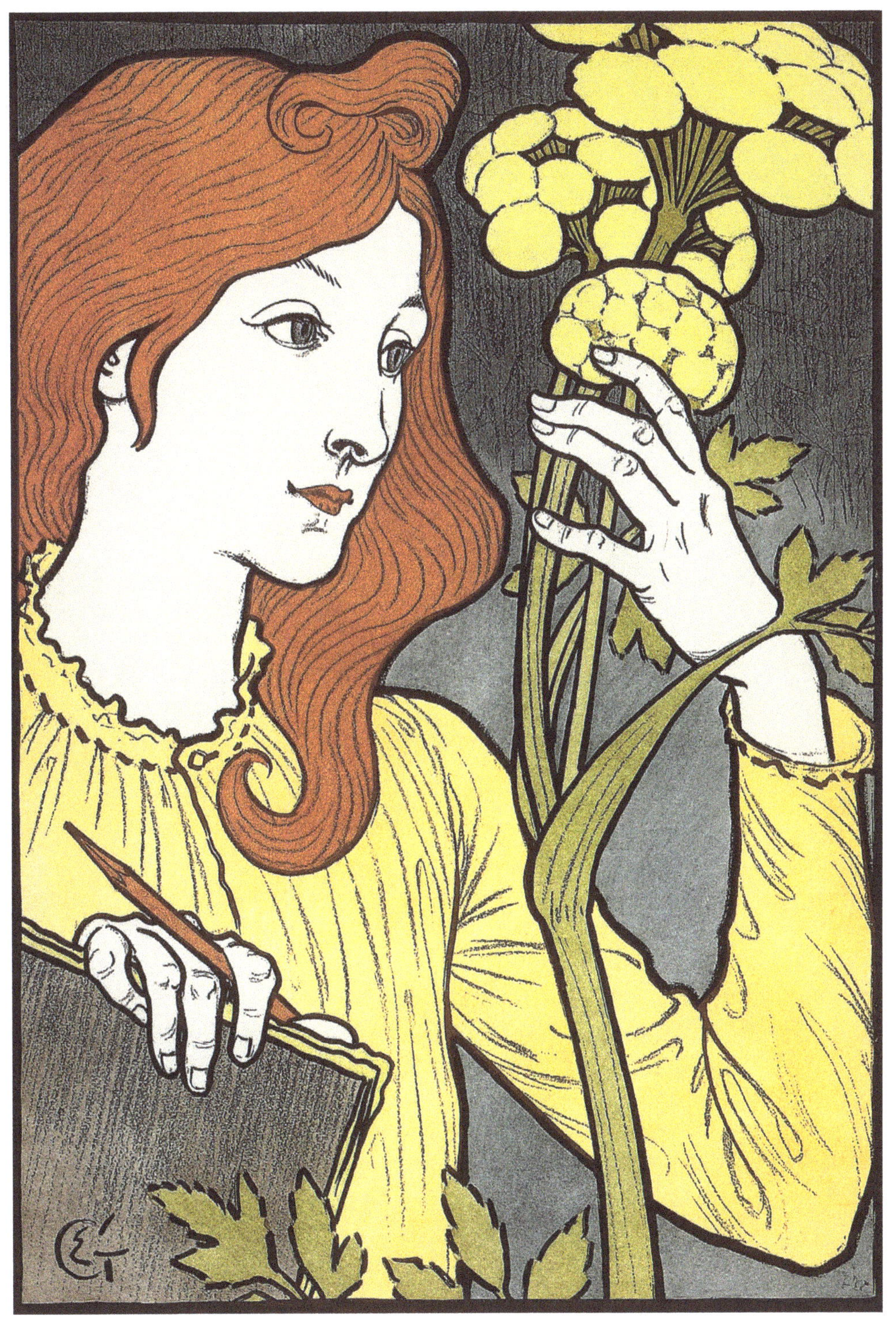

▲ **Eugène Grasset**, *Salon des cent*, 1894.
Print for a colour poster. Victor and Gretha Arwas collection.

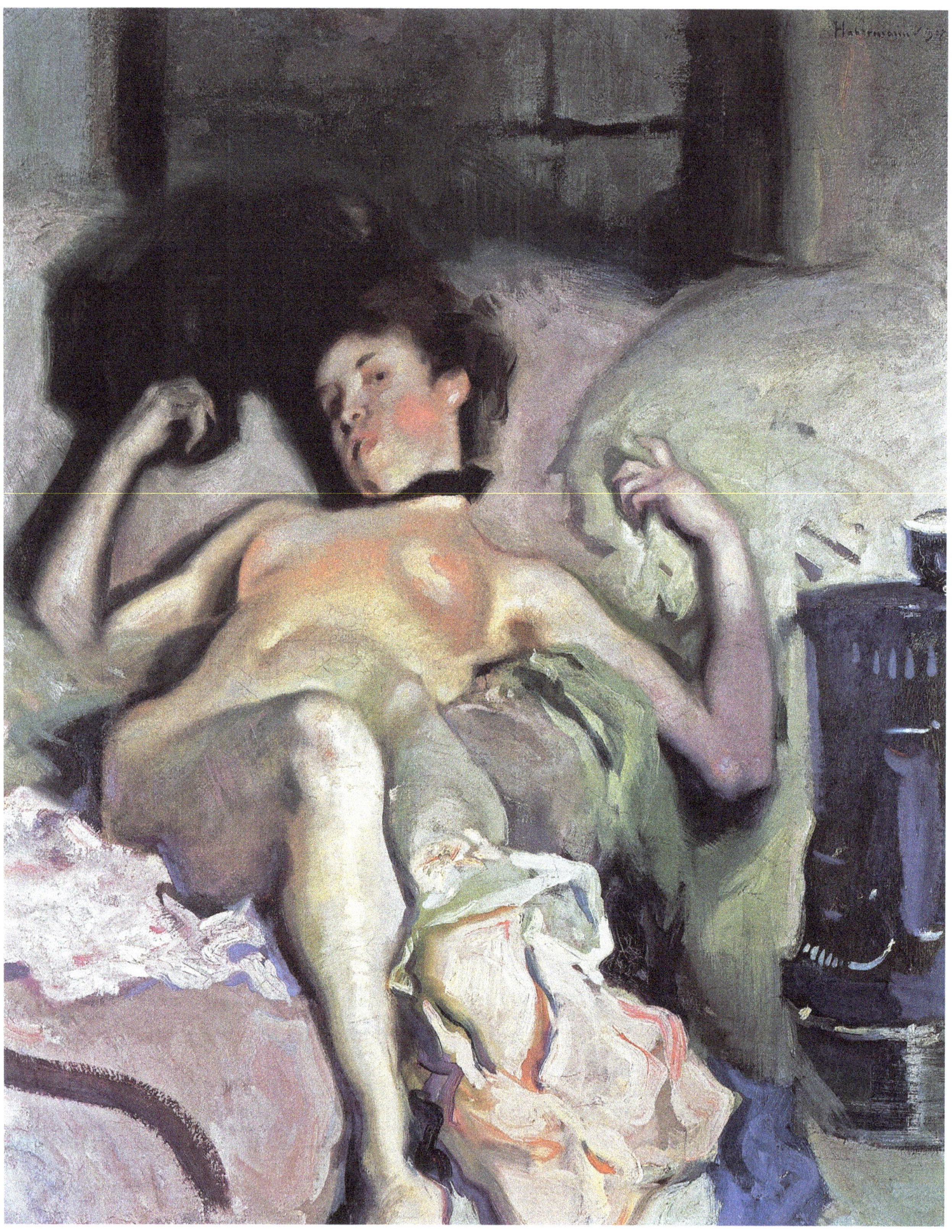

VIENNA AT THE TURN OF THE CENTURY

The two decades between 1885 and 1918 were a turbulent time of social and cultural paradigm shifts for Vienna, capital of a multi-ethnic empire on the verge of losing the pomp and glory of the 19th century. However, the creation of the Viennese Secession and the *Wiener Werkstätte* (Viennese Workshops) marked a leap into the modern age, at least culturally.

In 1861, the local artists had already joined the *Genossenschaft der bildenden Künstler Wiens* (Association of Fine Artists in Vienna) and found a home in the *Künstlerhaus*, a renaissance-style building designed by August Weber, that was situated directly at the main boulevard in Vienna. However, the building soon outgrew its initial conception and several additions had to be made: two wings in 1882 and a roof for the atrium in 1888. Nowadays the building houses several cultural venues, a cinema and theatre in the wings, as well as a modern Internet café. In the course of the 20th century it was on the verge of being demolished several times, but, nevertheless, survived and thrived and is today, thanks to a multitude of varying exhibitions, livelier than ever.

In the 19th century, the construction of the *Künstlerhaus* was just one of the many construction projects that were simultaneously commissioned and led to an economic upsurge in the city. Due to the high influx of unemployed workers and farmers from Bohemia and Moravia, another urban expansion (the first one was initiated in 1850) became necessary. This made Vienna the fourth-largest city in Europe with 800.000 inhabitants after London, Paris and Berlin. In the course of ten years the number of inhabitants doubled until it reached 2.000.000 in 1910, making Vienna the fourth-largest city in the world after New York, London, and Paris. For that reason, the urban expansion in the 1890s not only incorporated smaller boroughs surrounding but also included the construction of new districts and the subterranean diversion of the Vienna River. Already in 1897, the first electrical tram line was made operational, a belated successor to the Viennese horse-powered tram which was ferrying people from between 1840 and 1841 – long before Germany or Switzerland would establish a similar transportation system.

◀ **Hugo von Habermann**,
Reclining Nude, 1907.
Oil on canvas, 100.5 x 83 cm.
Bavarian State Painting Collection, Neue Pinakothek, Munich.

All these construction projects required an additional workforce. This led to a huge influx of workers from the eastern realms of the Austro-Hungarian Empire who were given work in the brickworks as unskilled labourers or construction workers. Not all of the immigrants, of whom great percentages were Jews from Eastern-European countries, were able to find work in the city. Together with sweeping industrialisation, the situation of the working class worsened as more and more craftspeople sank into poverty and thus into a lower social stratum. In turn, the conditions and the rising pressure to compete over jobs led to social tensions between the local population and the newly arrived groups from the same country, as well as to problems within these groups.

Some of the immigrant women could find much sought-after work as cooks or as maidservants in the employ of upper-class households. Naturally, those women who were working as cooks brought the culinary influences from their home countries with them, which gave the Viennese cuisine a distinct Czech nuance – surely not to the detriment of the local cuisine, which was already excellent.

In sum, Vienna became a cosmopolitan city and attracted a multitude of artists from all genres. However, the era of the great Viennese classical music that had seen geniuses like Joseph Haydn, Wolfgang Amadeus Mozart, Ludwig van Beethoven, and Franz Schubert, was drawing to an end. Especially the typically Viennese passion for the Waltz and the Opera, which was shaped by artists like Joseph Lanner, Johann Strauss I, Johann Strauss II, Oscar Strauss – not a relative of the famous Strauss family and almost but forgotten today – Karl Millöcker, Franz Lehar, Emmerich Kálmán, or Robert Stolz, was slowly fading.

As previously mentioned, the second half of the 19th century was characterised by a plethora of constructional activity in Vienna. In 1857, at the behest of Emperor Franz Joseph, the demolition of the medieval city wall that still surrounded the city centre was initiated. During this period, the *Ringstraßenviertel* was created: a thriving new district of magnificent buildings and beautiful parks, while the essence of regeneration provided Gustav Klimt and his partners with the opportunity to showcase their talent. The first commissions did not take long to follow, and they were asked to contribute artistically to the festivities on the occasion of the silver wedding of Emperor Franz Joseph and Empress Elisabeth. Shortly after that, they painted a ceiling fresco for a spa in Karlsbad. More state commissions followed. A study of Klimt's paintings of that time – like *Fable* (1883) or *The Idyll* (1884) – reveals that, although he was a talented and promising young artist, his art was rooted in the conventional, academic standards for allegorical and mythological themes.

The colours in *The Idyll* are not particularly elegant but still skilfully colour the fabrics of the central figure with her smooth hair. She would neither have been shocking nor inspiring in the 17th or 18th century. Her beauty is rather maternal and matronesque while her nakedness is more decorative than arousing. In the past the pubic region was – if at all – stylised to a smooth, innocent "V". Numerous paintings from early

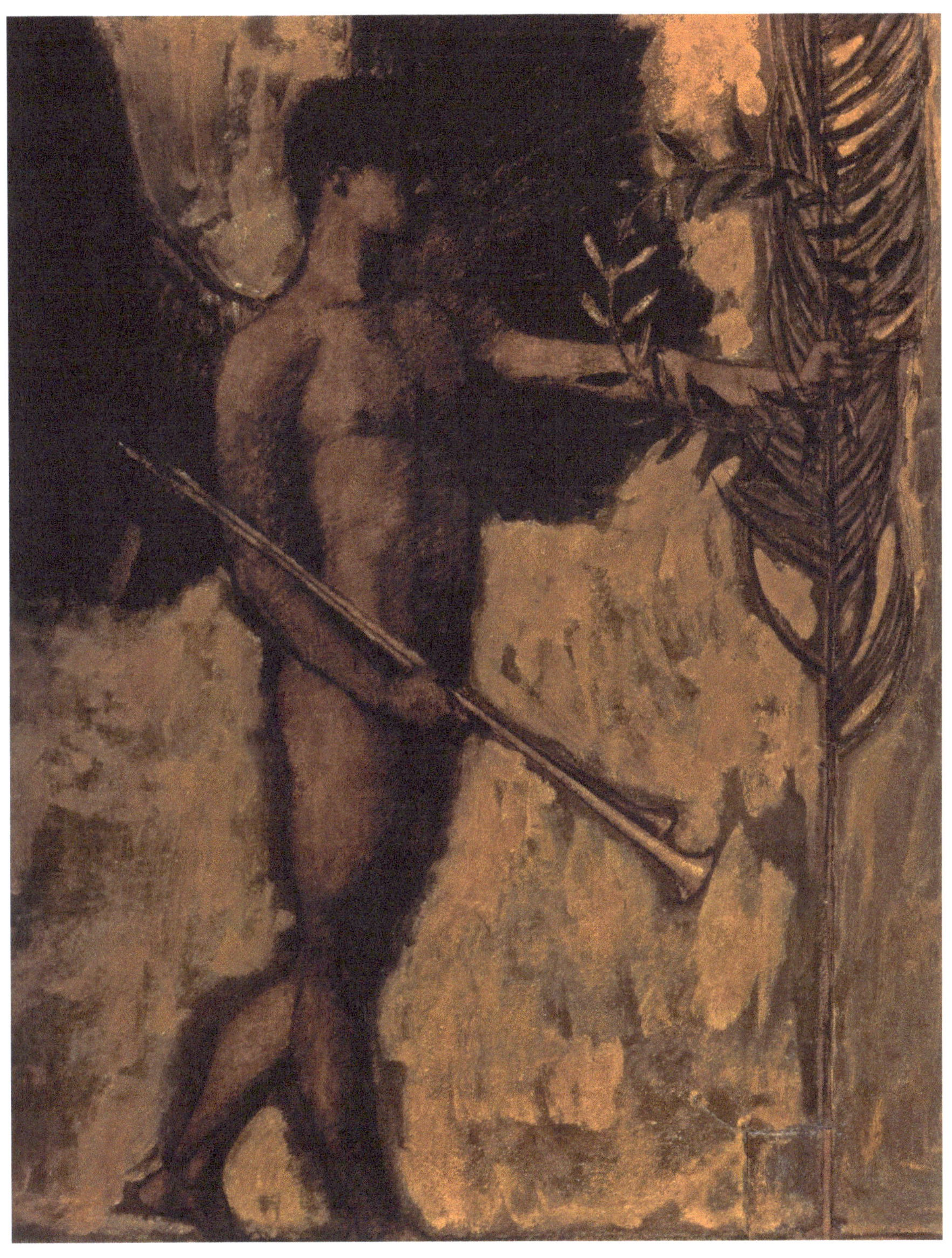

▲ **Franz von Stuck**, *Poster draft for the First International Exhibition of Art, "Homage to painting", at the Glaspalast (detail)*, 1899. Mixed technique on cardboard. Museum Villa Stuck, Munich.

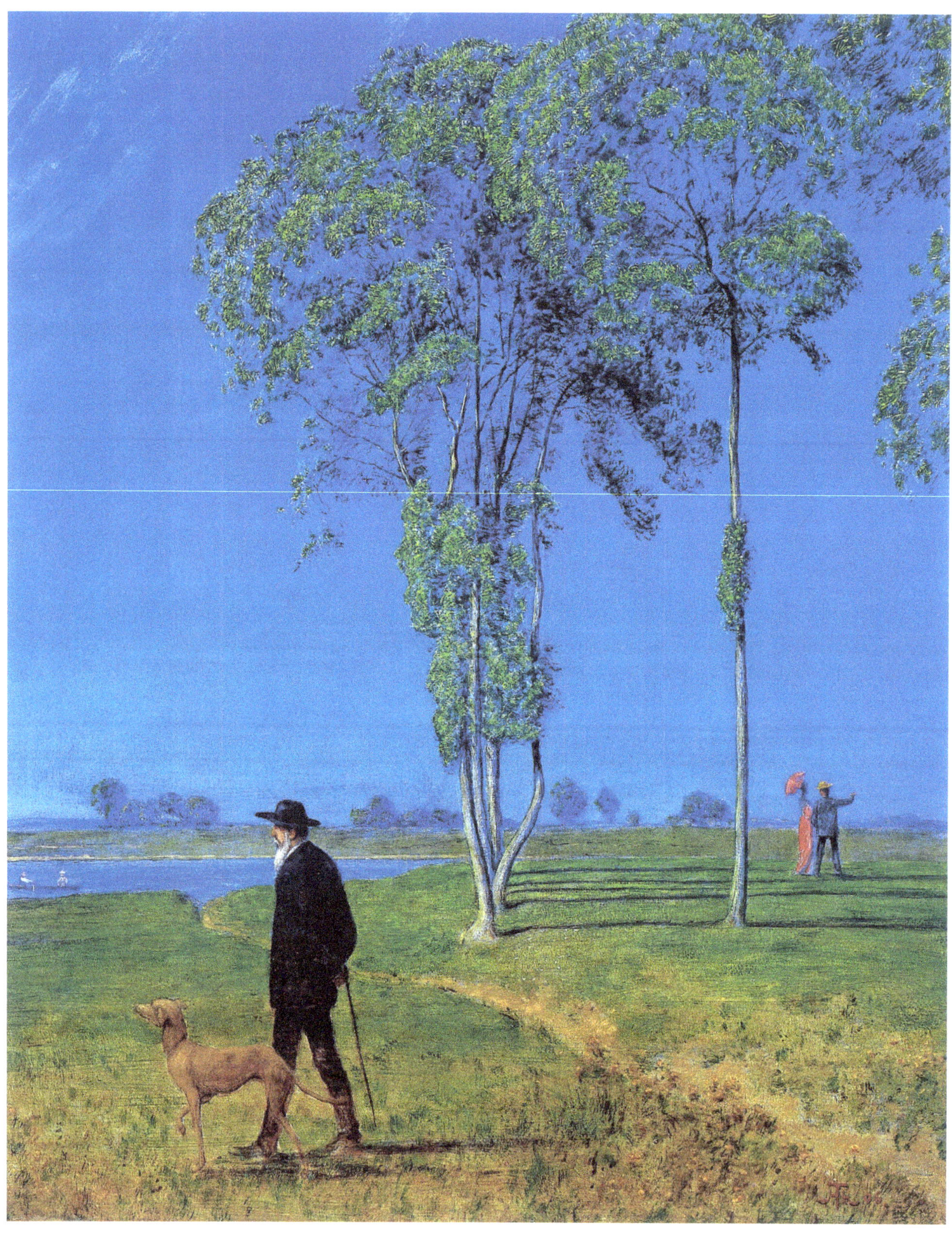

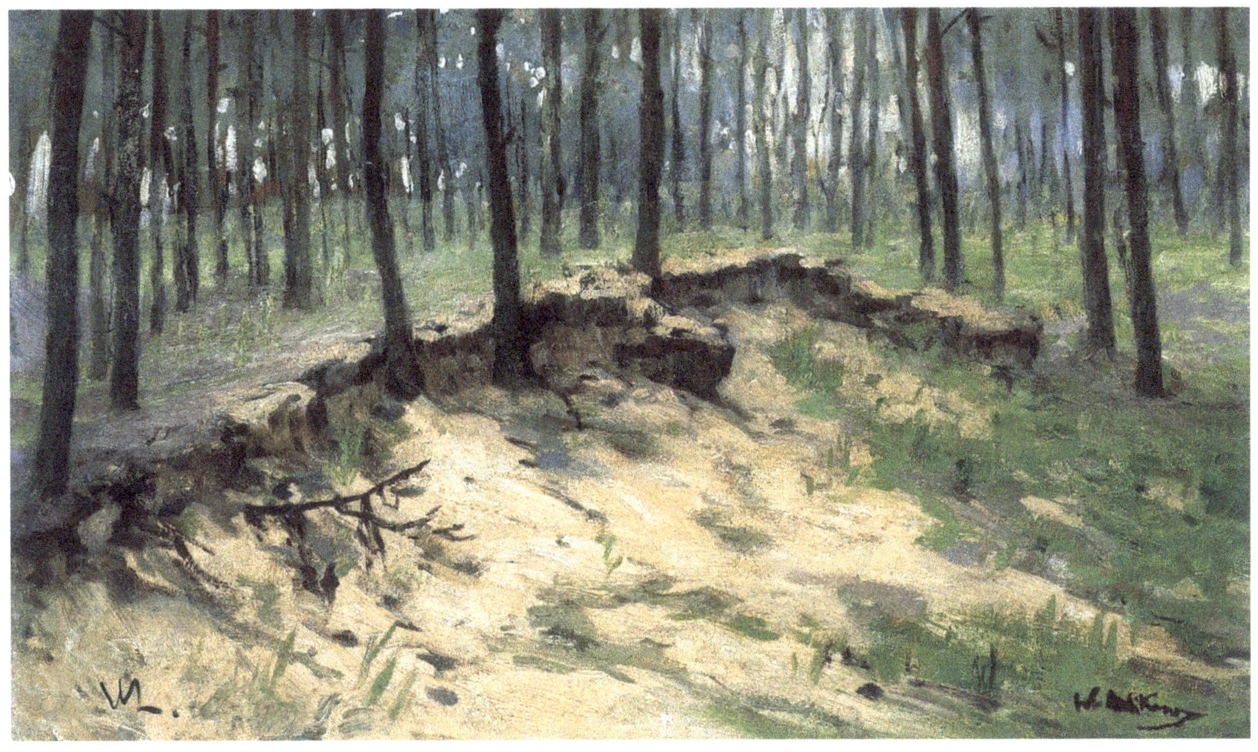

◀ **Hans Thoma**,
Solitude, 1906.
Oil on canvas, 82 x 67 cm.
Landesbank Baden-Württemberg Collection.

Walter Leistikow, ▲
Waldstück mit Sandgrube (Corner of Forest with Sand Pit), c. 1905.
Oil on canvas, 30 x 50 cm.
Staatliche Museen zu Berlin, Berlin.

medieval times or the early Renaissance who dared to show or allude to male or female genitalia were later covered with absurd fig leaves.

By 1896, Klimt already began painting the human body in a more unconventional and individual manner. For example, there is an interesting discrepancy between the last study for *Allegory of Sculpture* and the fully realised painting: in the study, the wild and loose hair that would later characterise Klimt's style is already visible and there are traces of a more detailed depiction of pubic hair. The woman is looking directly at the viewer and strikes a provocative pose, as if she was caught naked in her bedroom. The painting, on the contrary, shows a traditional figure again: her pose is classically sculpture-like, her hair is braided and the pubic hair is gone.

All the early commissions made Klimt a successful and popular artist. In 1892, Klimt's father died, shortly followed by his brother Ernst. In that difficult time, the relationship between Klimt and his co-student Franz Matsch, with whom he and his brother Ernst had founded the *Künstler-Compagnie*, cooled off. These events deeply impacted Klimt and he began to forge new and more adventurous paths.

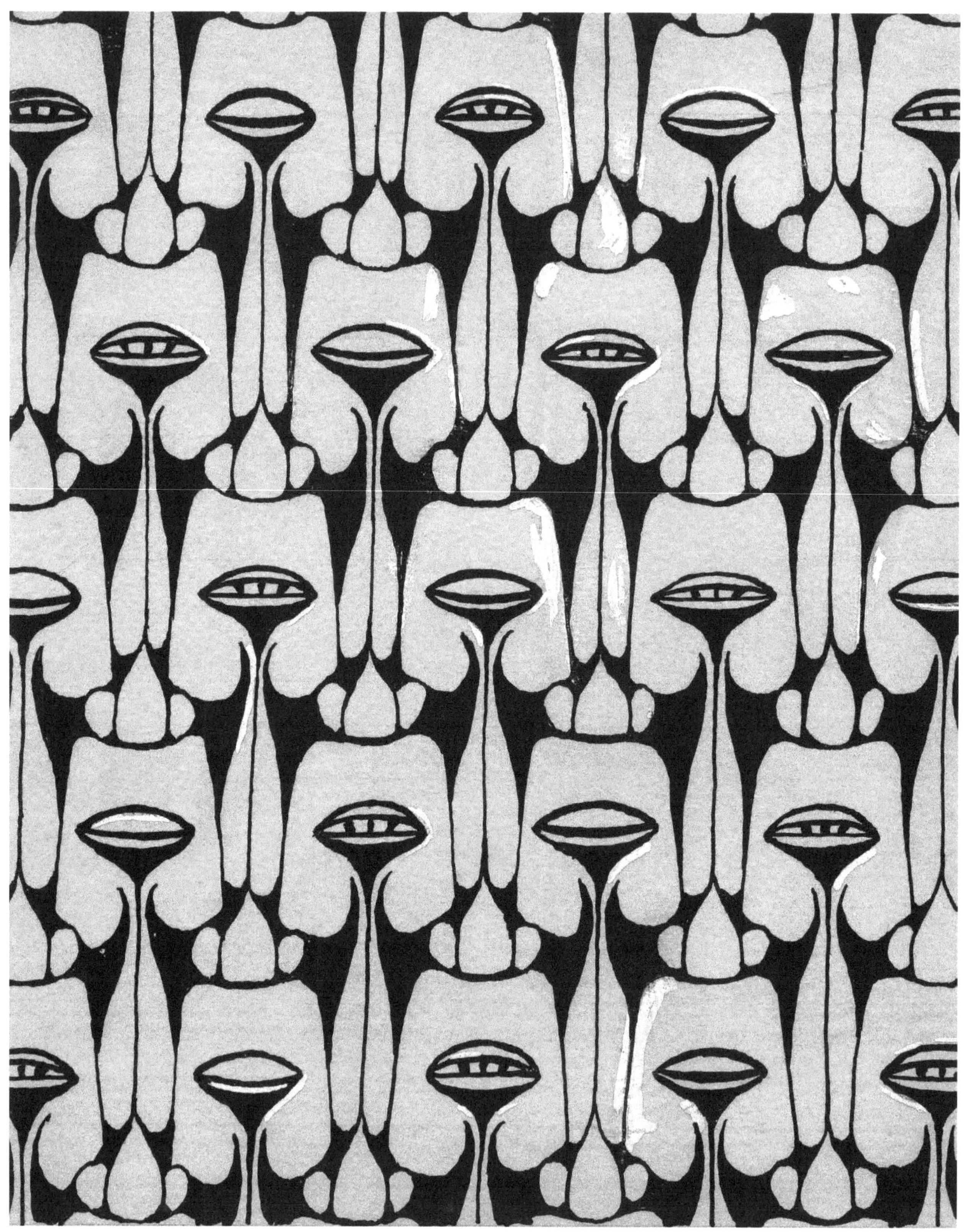

THE SECESSION

Apart from Gustav Klimt and Franz Matsch, many other artists participated in the beginning of the movement: Wilhelm List, Carl Moll, Ernst Stöhr, Max Kurzweil, Koloman Moser, and Josef Engelhart. This core group essentially founded in 1897 the Vienna Secession after a coffee-house meeting. Later, the architects Josef Hoffmann, who was also one of the co-founders of the *Wiener Werkstätte* (*Vienna's Workshops*), and Josef Maria Olbrich joined the illustrious group as well. Gustav Klimt, barely aged 35, took up the presidency. Soon a motto was found as well: "Every era needs its own art and all art needs its freedom."

Thus, program and mission statement for the movement were set for the forty members who were all already established artists. In practice, their motto could also have been "Art for everyone and for every stratum of society." During this decade, Vienna was basically obsessed with aesthetics and eroticism. It was an era of happiness, craze and a flurry of intellectual activity. The Secessionists were searching for new artistic expressions, had developed their own ideal of beauty and wanted to steer their movement into a direction that did not require submission to political, economical or financial constraints; in essence, they wanted a "typically Austrian *Jugendstil*".

As to satisfy the conditions of etiquette and formality, they drafted a letter of termination to the *Genossenschaft der bildenden Künstler Wiens im Künstlerhaus*:

> The board of directors is probably aware that a group of artists within the organisation has been trying to make themselves and their artistic ideas heard for years. These ideas now culminate in the realisation of a necessity: the necessity to establish contact between the artistic scene in Vienna and the ever-progressing art scene outside of Austria. Furthermore exhibitions need to be freed of commercial interests and organised

◀ **Koloman Moser**,
Pattern for the cover of Ver Sacrum (detail), 1899.
Collection and Archive, Universität für angewandte Kunst, Vienna.

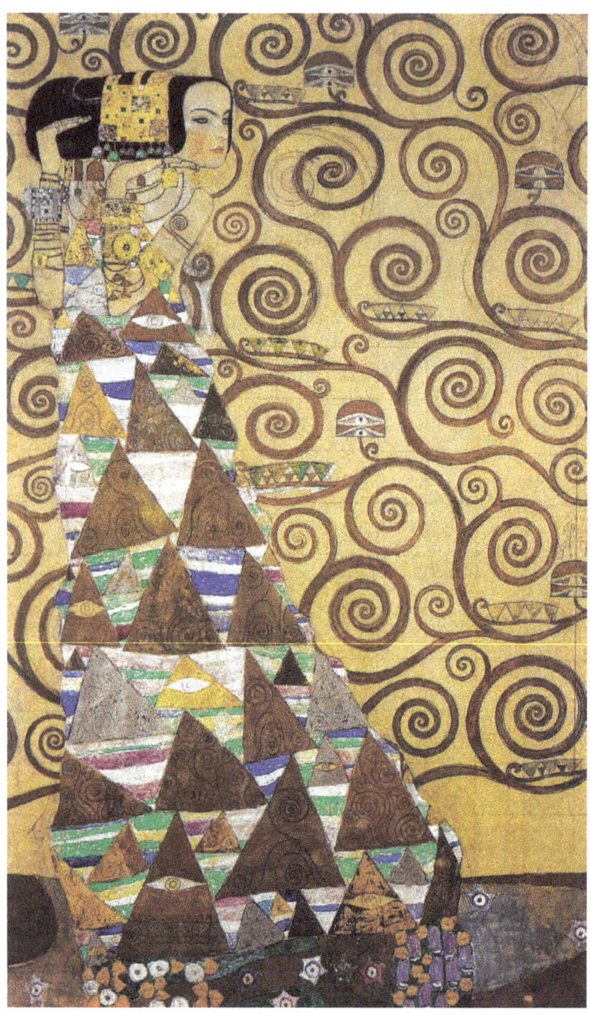

according to purely artistic standards, so that a pure and modern concept of art can be taught to the broader public. Finally, a higher understanding of art needs to be awakened in higher circles.

Klimt, Moll, and Hoffmann were responsible for the organisation of exhibitions until 1905. This function in the Secession naturally furthered Klimt's reputation, which led to him gaining more influence at the Imperial court, with the government and his colleagues. The Secession was ultimately successful in finding wealthy patrons and securing subsidies for their fledgling association. They received commissions from museums, theatres, and other official institutions. However, first and foremost the founders of the movement had several specific objectives they wanted to accomplish: to help young artists exhibit their work; invite the best foreign artists to Vienna; publish a distinctive and original art magazine; and finally elevate the artistic standard in Vienna to an international level.

For that reason, four non-resident artists were invited into the Secession: Fernand Khnopff from Belgium, Max Klinger from Germany, the Swiss artist Ferdinand Hodler, and Jan Toorop from the Netherlands.

Gustav Klimt, ▶
Accomplishment, c.1905-1909.
Cardboard for the Stoclet Frieze, 194.6 x 120.3 cm.
Österreichisches Museum, Vienna.

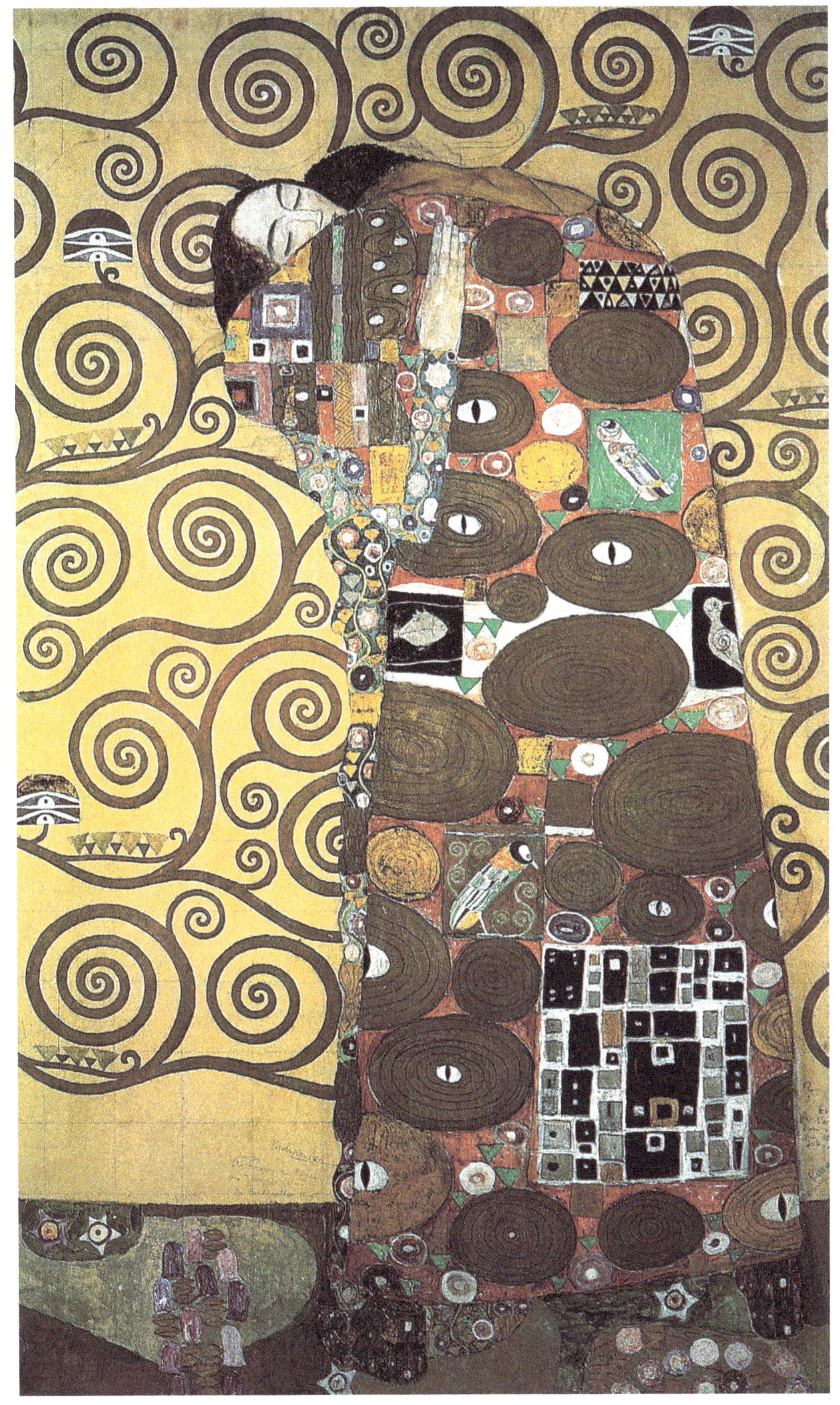

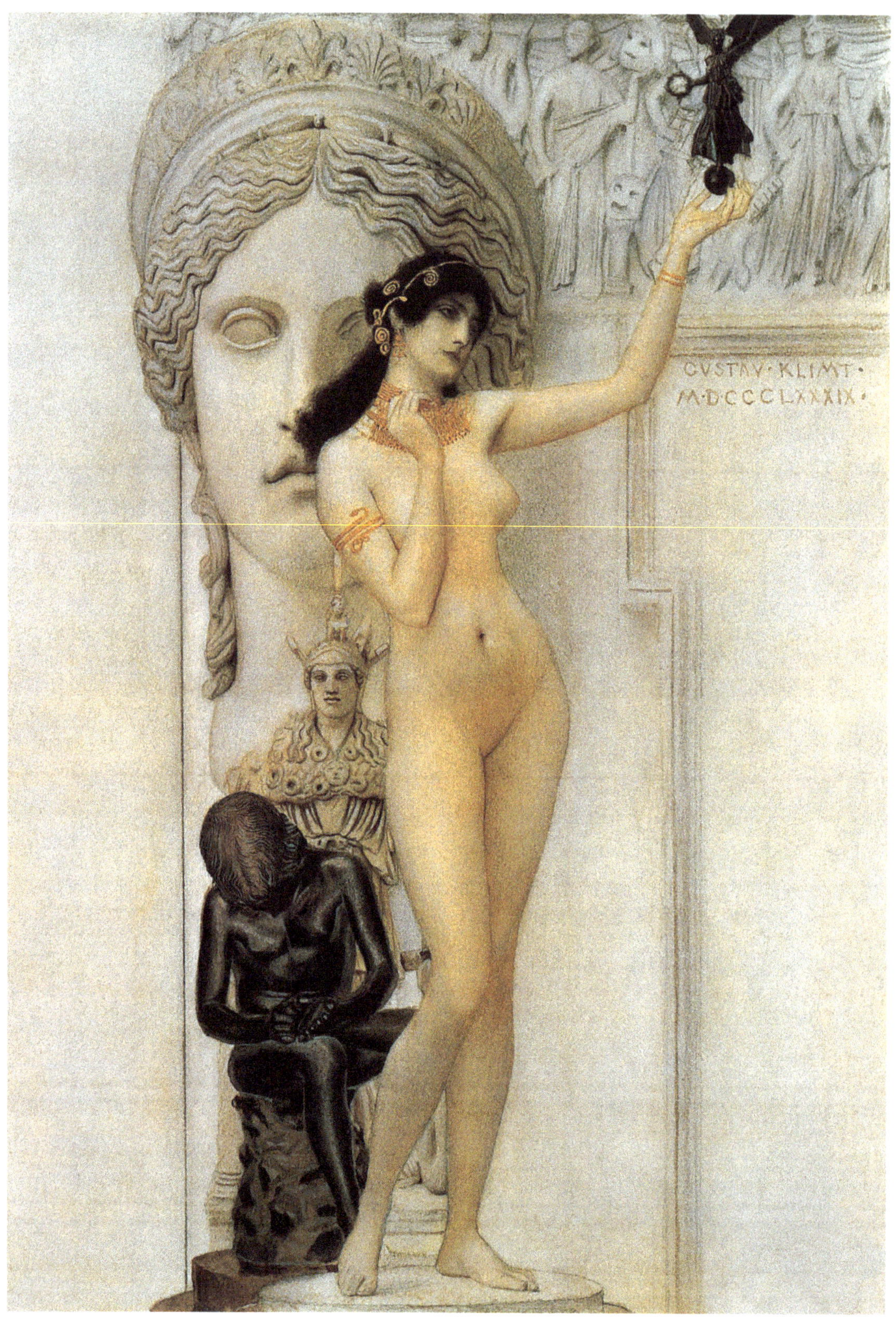

GVSTAV · KLIMT ·
M · D · C · C · C · L · X · X · X · I X ·

THE *VER SACRUM* MAGAZINE

The Viennese Secession soon had its own statutes but more importantly a mouth piece with the official magazine of the Vienna Secession *Ver Sacrum* (Latin for "sacred spring"), which was published from 1898 to 1903. It took its name possibly from either one of these two sources: Some art historians think that it was inspired by an old Roman ritual, dedicated to their gods, meant to celebrate the foundation of a new township while others assume that the name was borrowed from Ludwig Uhland's poem *Der Weihefrühling* (*The Sacred Spring*). Artists from the Secession contributed to the magazine along with popular local writers and other foreign artists.

The magazine, under the directorship of Wilhelm List, had a print run of five years (1898-1903) and had a limited publication of 300 copies per issue. In the first two years the magazine was published monthly, then bimonthly in 1901. One of the most prolific contributors was Klimt, who regularly wrote articles for *Ver Sacrum.* The publication was highly regarded – from a literary and artistic point of view – and had a high influence on Austrian and foreign artists.

Hermann Bahr penned the most important principle of the Secession: "*We want art that is not a slave to foreign influences but at the same time is neither afraid nor hateful of them.*"

Despite all the praise there were also problems with the magazine. One of the issues was confiscated by a district attorney because it "abrasively violated the sense of shame with its depiction of nudity and thus created public outrage". Klimt responded to these charges that he did not want to deal with boorish people and that it was more important to him that there were people who liked the drawing. He was referring to his private patronage, his clients from the ranks of the Viennese upper class.

In the course of five years 70 issues were published, which had a purely didactic role and were often dedicated to one specific topic per issue. For example, one special issue was dedicated to Jan Toorop, whose symbolic picture language was a great influence on

◀ **Gustav Klimt**,
Allegory of Sculpture, 1889.
Pencil and watercolour, 44 x 30 cm.
Wien Museum Karlplatz, Vienna.

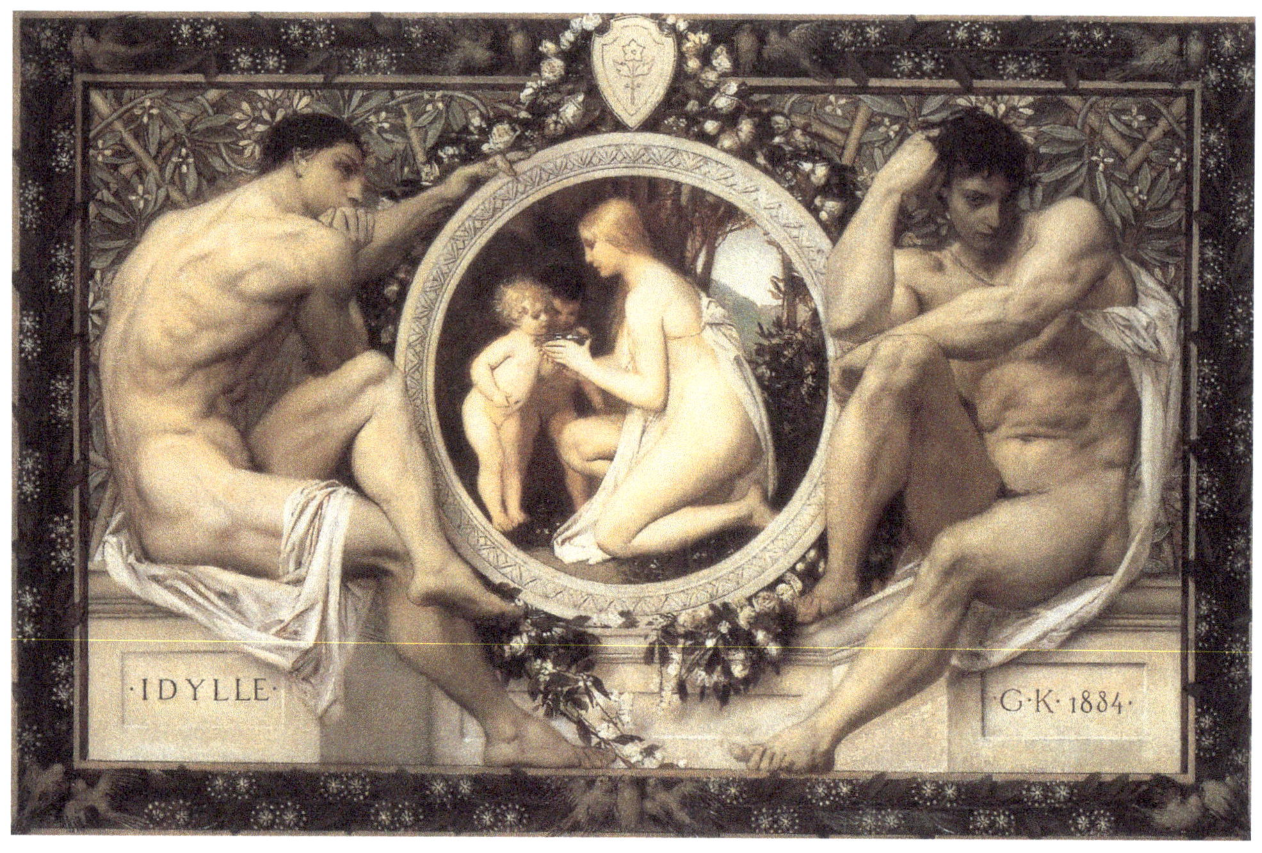

▲ **Gustav Klimt**,
The Idyll, 1884.
Oil on canvas, 50 x 74 cm.
Wien Museum Karlplatz, Vienna.

Gustav Klimt, ▶
Poster for the First Secession Exhibition, 1898 (before censure).
Lithograph, 63.5 x 46.9 cm.
Neue Galerie, New York.

Klimt. Another complete issue was dedicated to Khnopff-reproductions while the November issue of 1899 was an essay written by Belgian poet Emile Verhaeren about the oeuvre of the Flemish painter Theo van Rysselberghe.

Ver Sacrum propagated the idea of holistic art, which stated that all art needs to form a synthesis and can thus be appreciated by everyone: the poor and the rich, the powerful and the powerless. The content varied between essays about art theory and practical, visual examples. Often the issues contained original prints. The magazine appeared roughly at the same time as another important magazine that was published beyond the Alps, in Munich, and was called *Die Jugend (The Youth)*. The Munich magazine marked the beginning of the local *Jugendstil*-movement and was essentially the inspiration for their name.

In 1903, *Ver Sacrum* and discontinued due to a lack of subscribers.

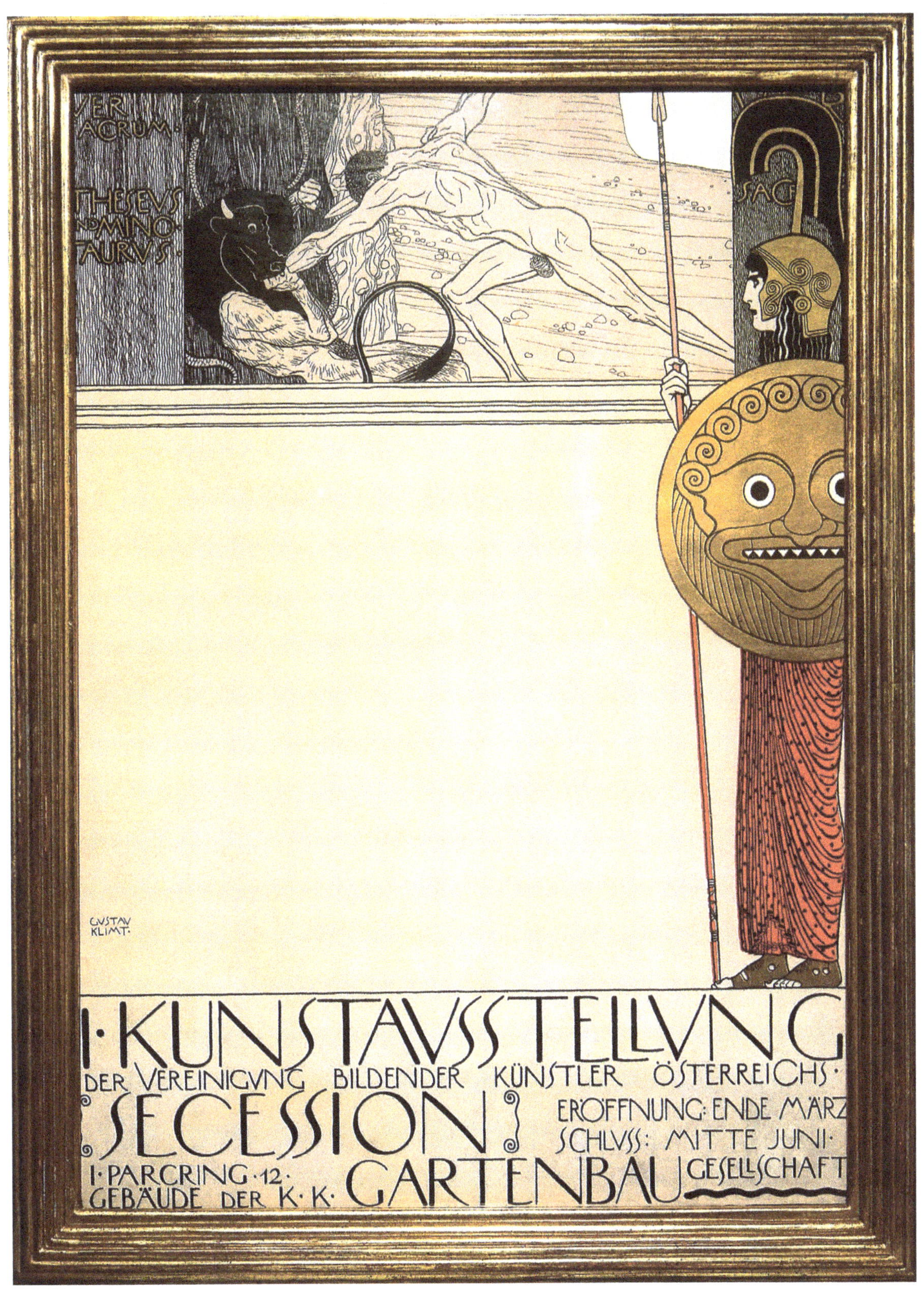

VER
ACRVM
THESEVS
Σ MINO
TAVRVS
SACR
I · KVNSTAVSSTELLVNG
DER VEREINIGVNG BILDENDER KÜNSTLER ÖSTERREICHS ·
SECESSION
ERÖFFNVNG: ENDE MÄRZ
SCHLVSS: MITTE JUNI ·
I · PARCRING · 12 ·
GEBÄVDE DER K · K · GARTENBAV GESELLSCHAFT
GVSTAV KLIMT ·

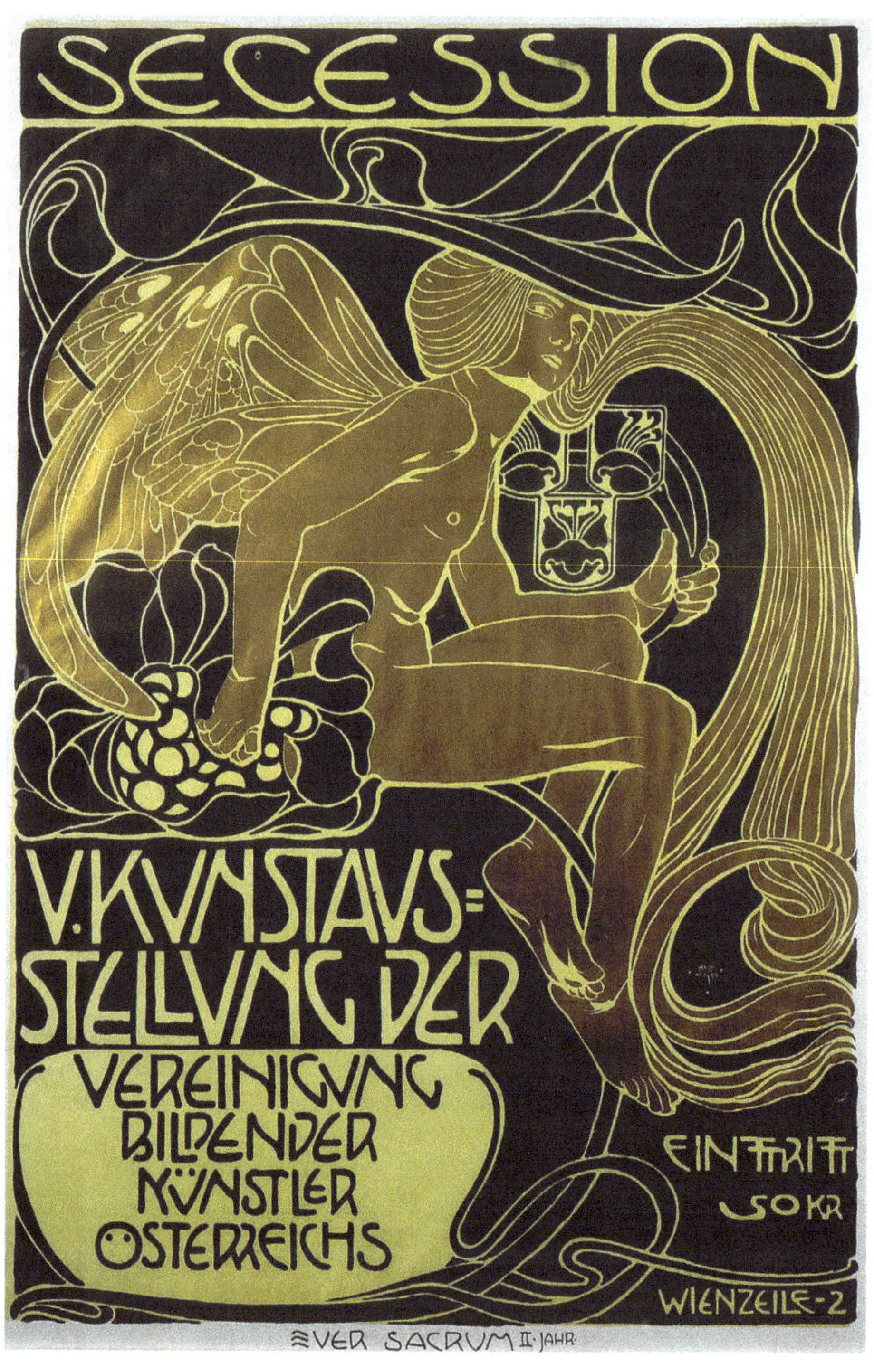

▲ **Koloman Moser**, *Poster for the Fifth Secession Exhibition,* 1899.
Coloured lithograph on paper, 100 x 69.5 cm. Wien Museum, Vienna.

THE EXHIBITION CENTRE OF THE VIENNESE SECESSION

At least the early work of the Secessionists was meant to provoke and cause outrage; an idea they were successful with. Ludwig Hevesi associated the architectural style of the Secession building, with its unusual oriental influences, with "the golden backdrop of medieval times". Vienna's citizens, however, mocked the building and called it "the Temple of the Three Frogs" or "The Tomb of Mahdi" or – even worse – "The Crematorium" and "The Mausoleum". The dome was generally referred to as "the cabbage head". Hermann Bahr spoke quite differently about the building in an article in October 1898:

> [...] the building is the new house of the Secession and has been designed by the young architect Olbrich. On the 4th of November it is meant to become municipal. The same day will see the start of its first exhibition. I suspect that there will be a great outcry and the foolish people will rage. That is why I want to say the most important things right now, while I am calm and dispassionate. Polemics will come later.

After leaving the first room, we enter the building itself. Everything is functional here. There is no frivolous attempt to boast or to blind with pomp. The house of the Secession does not want to be a palace or a temple but rather a room that is able to arrange works of art to best effect possible. The artist did not ask himself, "How can I design this so that it looks the most impressive?" but rather "How can this serve its purpose, its new mission, our needs?" [....]

Josef Hoffmann, who played an important role in the shaping of aesthetic perception and the study and understanding of aesthetics in the 20th century, also contributed to the success of the first exhibition. As a dedication to him, visitors of the second exhibition could read the following text in the catalogue:

> *"May the words of Hevesi, as they are written above our building, become true – Every era needs its art and all art needs its freedom" [...].*

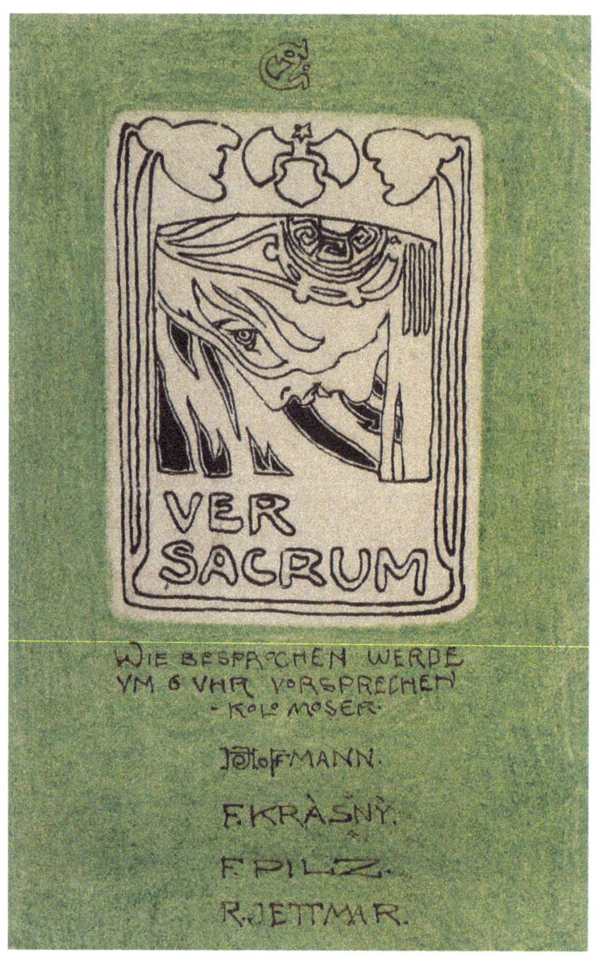

▲ **Koloman Moser,**
Postcard to Carl Moll with Ver Sacrum sketch, 1897.
Pen and coloured pencil on paper, 9 x 14 cm.
Private collection, Vienna.

The Viennese Secession differed in certain respects from the *Jugendstil*-movement. They used decorative elements that were directly derived from nature, like leaves, animals, or grapevine shoots. The floral elements often included three-dimensional adornments like snakes or salamanders. This association of arts was not only exclusive to painters as their membership was founded on the concept of holistic art. They were comprised of designers, architects, artisans, and painters who wanted to unite all aspects of life into one comprehensive artwork.

The sixth exhibition in 1900 was dedicated to Japanese art and Japonism as a European-born, Japanese-influenced branch of art. In essence, it was a time of awakening for all arts. For the 13th exhibition in 1902 – which 21 artists enriched with their contributions – Klimt created the *Beethoven Frieze*, an allegorical painting portraying man's search for happiness, inspired by Beethoven's last symphony. The 9th symphony in itself was a novelty in the history of music, as the movement required soloists and a mixed choir. Later, in 1985, this last movement – combined with Friedrich Schiller's poem *Ode to Joy* – would be chosen as the hymn for the European Union. Max Klinger also contributed to the Beethoven-theme with his sculpture *Beethoven*. Both works of art have come to symbolise the Viennese Secession.

Koloman Moser, ▶
*Poster design for the "First Grand Art Exhibition" of the
Viennese Secession,* 1897.
Watercolour, gouache, coloured pencil, metal colour on
tracing linen, 78.5 x 60.5 cm.
Leopold Museum, Vienna.

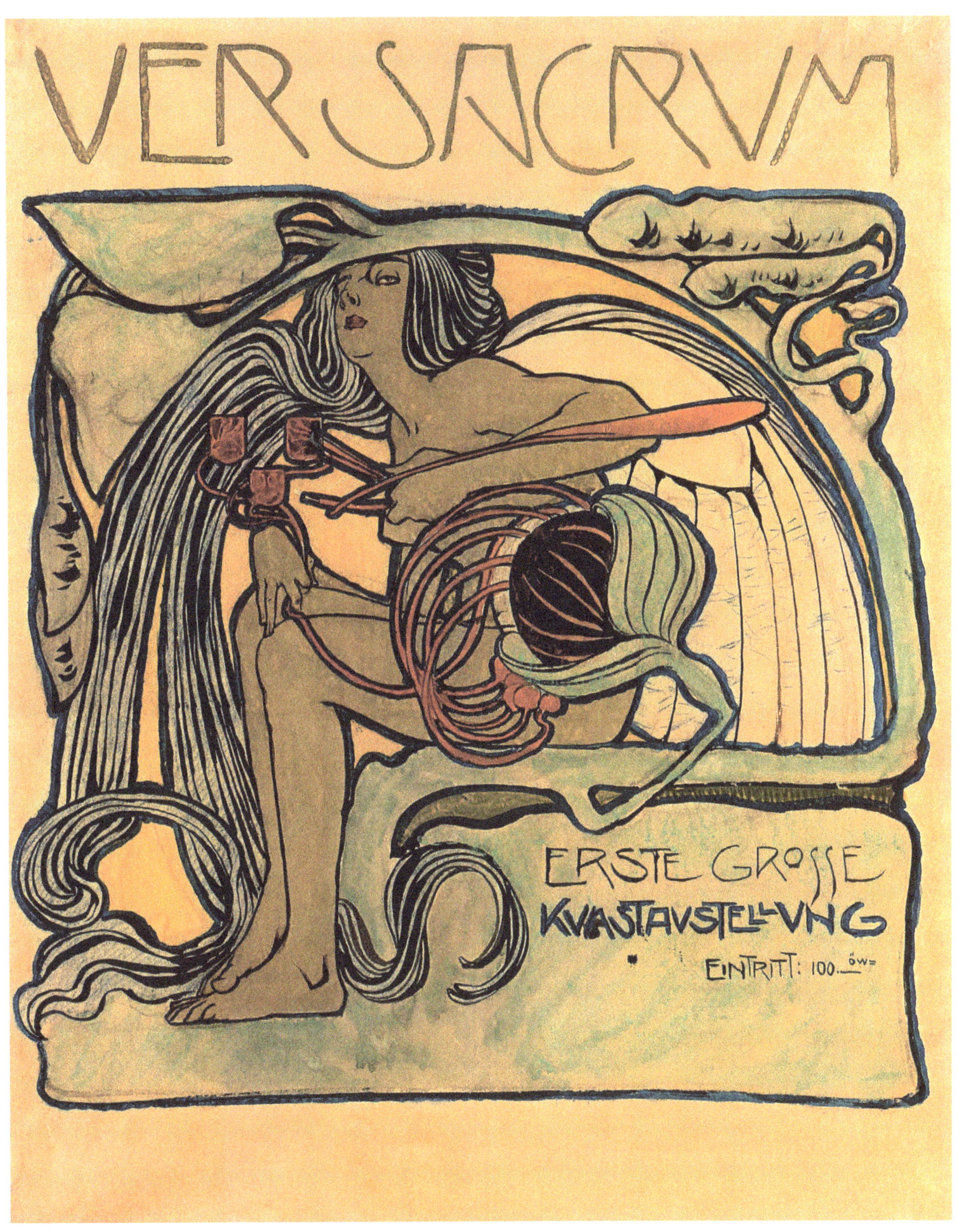

VER SACRVM
ERSTE GROSSE
KVNSTAVSTELLVNG
EINTRITT: 100.öw=

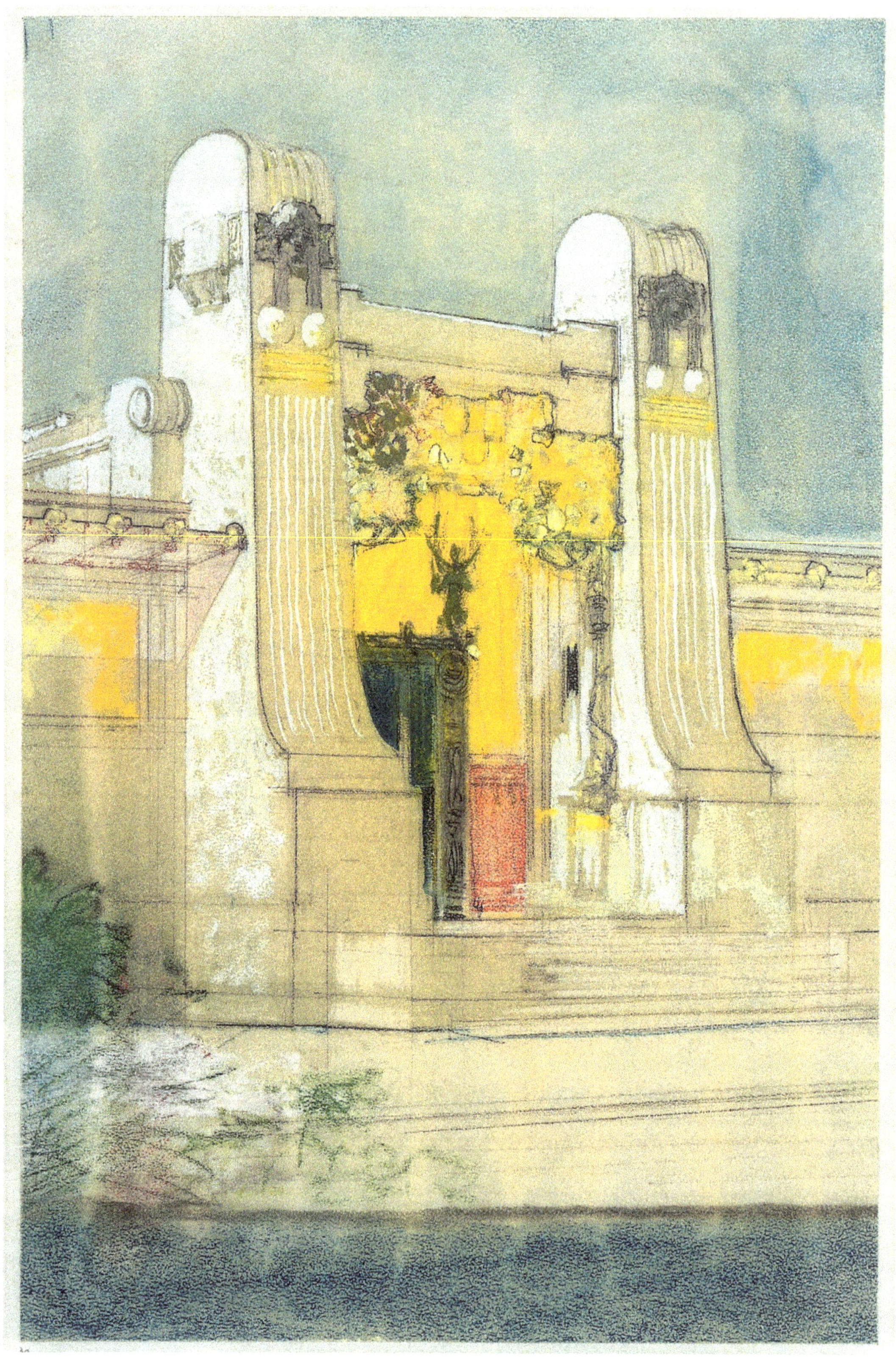

THE BEETHOVEN FRIEZE

Klimt's painting cycle *Beethoven Frieze* was, together with Klinger's sculpture, a grand homage to the composer who lived and worked in Vienna until his death on 26 March 1827. He had been one of the most celebrated pianists and composers of his time. During the exhibition, the frieze was spread over three different walls and arranged sequentially in the left wing of the Secession-house. The individual paintings are categorised according to their order on the walls. First come *Floating Genii*, *Suffering Humanity*, and *Knight in Shining Armour*. The second wall showed *Hostile Forces*, *The Gorgons*, and the giant *Typhoeus*. The third wall showed *Poetry*, *The Arts*, and *Choir of Angels*.

The *Beethoven Frieze* was intended as a backdrop for Max Klinger's coloured, three-metre high sculpture. Since most of the ceiling frescoes in the

University of Vienna were destroyed, the frieze is the most important survivor. The huge and fragile painting – it was painted on plaster – survived miraculously, although it was initially not meant to be a permanent installation. This is a small comfort for the other art losses that the world of art suffered as a consequence of World War II.

With 56,000 visitors and sales amounting to 85,000 *Kronen*, the Beethoven-exhibition established itself instantly as an influential element in Austria. Even the omnipresent ruler of the Austro-Hungarian Empire, Kaiser Franz Joseph I, was among the visitors. To honour the success of the exhibition, the emperor bestowed the golden order of merit upon Klimt. The eighth issue of *Ver Sacrum* published the results of the sales: 218 paintings.

In 1905, Klimt resigned as director of the Secession after long-running, irreconcilable conflicts with other members of the group. An untraversable chasm had opened between two parties within the association: the artists surrounding Klimt and the artists who wanted to focus solely on painting. The "Klimt Group" wanted to further applied arts like architecture

◀ **Joseph Maria Olbrich**,
Draft for the exhibition building of the Viennese Secession, perspective, 1897.
Pencil, charcoal, coloured pencil and opaque colour on light brown drawing board, 44.9 x 29.9 cm.
Library of Art, Staatliche Museen zu Berlin, Berlin.
Photograph by Dietmar Katz.

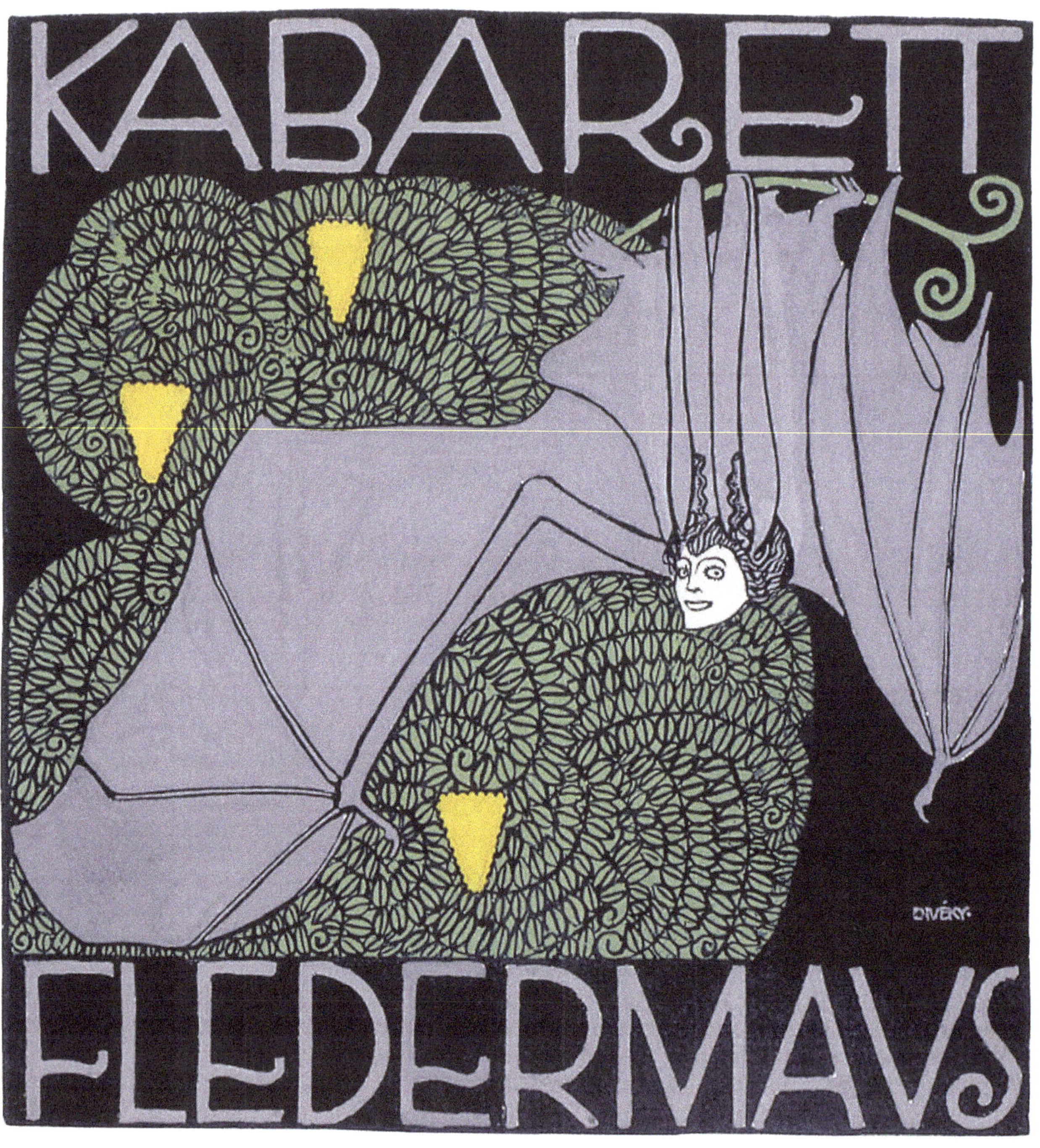

KABARETT
FLEDERMAVS
DIVÉKY

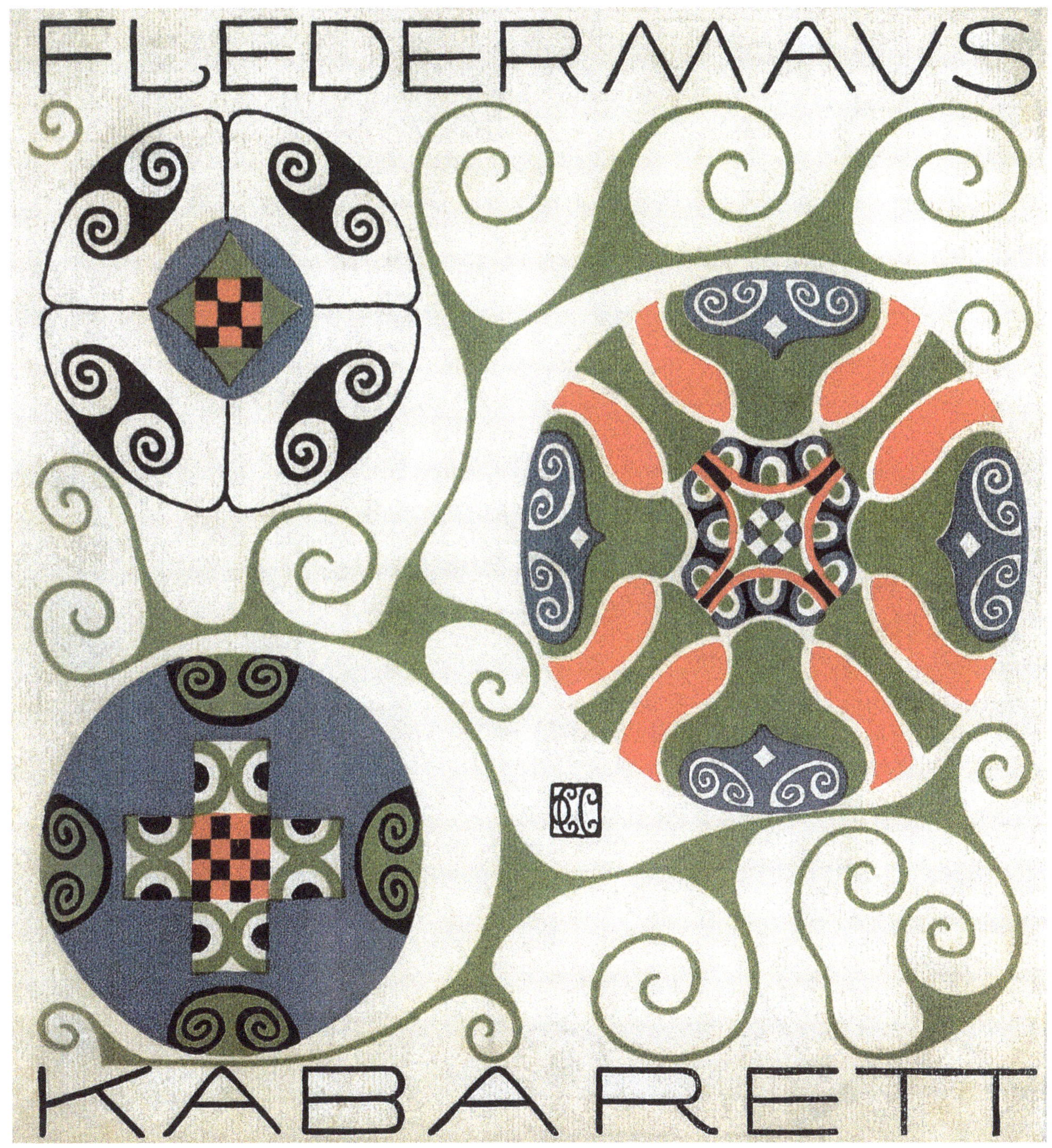
FLEDERMAVS
KABARETT

and design while the others wanted to improve the art of painting by making it the sole concern of the Secession. The dream of the Secession, to create harmony between the arts and thus deliver the world through art, had proven itself to be an unattainable Utopia.

How did contemporary witness Hermann Bahr judge the history of the Secession? He had already voiced his concerns five years earlier:

> What is it that the Secession originally wanted? What was its purpose? What did the young artists think when they left the old association? People said that they are against old art and for a new art. They were called all manner of names like symbolists or naturalists. Well, we have left those stupid words behind nowadays. Now we know that it is not about "old" or "new" or a specific school of painting, which they did not want to destroy everything that came before them or even that they wanted to establish a certain technique or way of seeing as scales to measure artists against. There are no old or new artists. There are artists and – let's say – makers.

> Artists are those who possess their own perception of the world, the people and life in general, and have the gift to share these impressions with others. Makers are those who just create without perceiving anything but have considerable talent to imitate the impressions of others. That is at the heart of the argument that has been running for so many years –in literature as well as in art. People argued against the process of just "making", against the absence of impressions and emotion, against the empty routine [...].

This shows that there were imitators who wanted to jump on the sudden success bandwagon and profit from the work of other artists.

Josef von Divéky, ▲
Poster design for the Cabaret Fledermaus, 1907.
Collection and Archive, Universität für angewandte Kunst, Vienna.

Carl Otto Czeschka, ▲
First Cabaret Fledermaus program (title-page), 1907.
Leopold Museum, Vienna.

Gustav Klimt, ▶
The Beethoven Frieze: The Three Gorgons (central panel, detail), 1902.
Casein on plaster, height: 220 cm.
Secession Hall, Vienna.

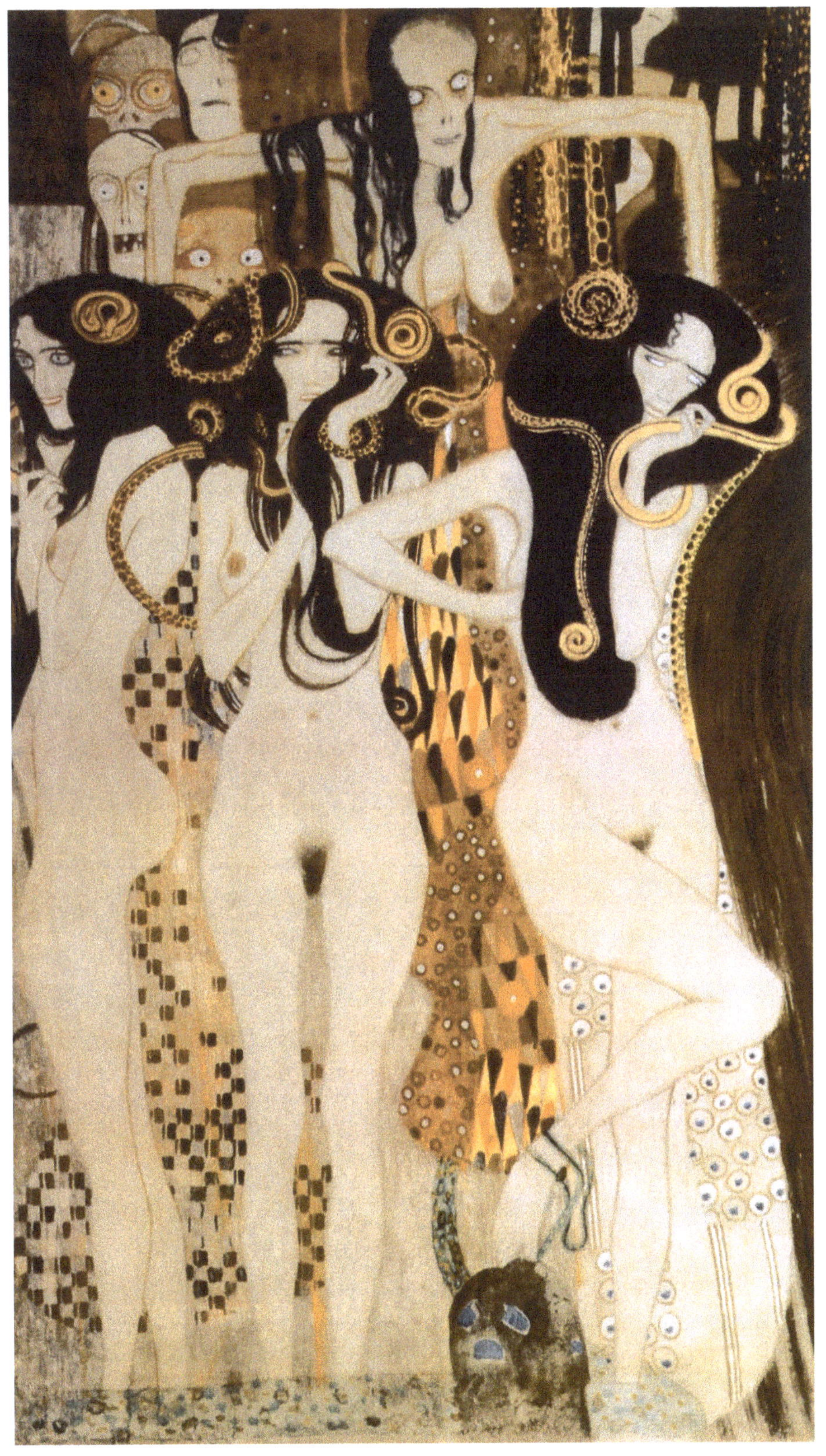

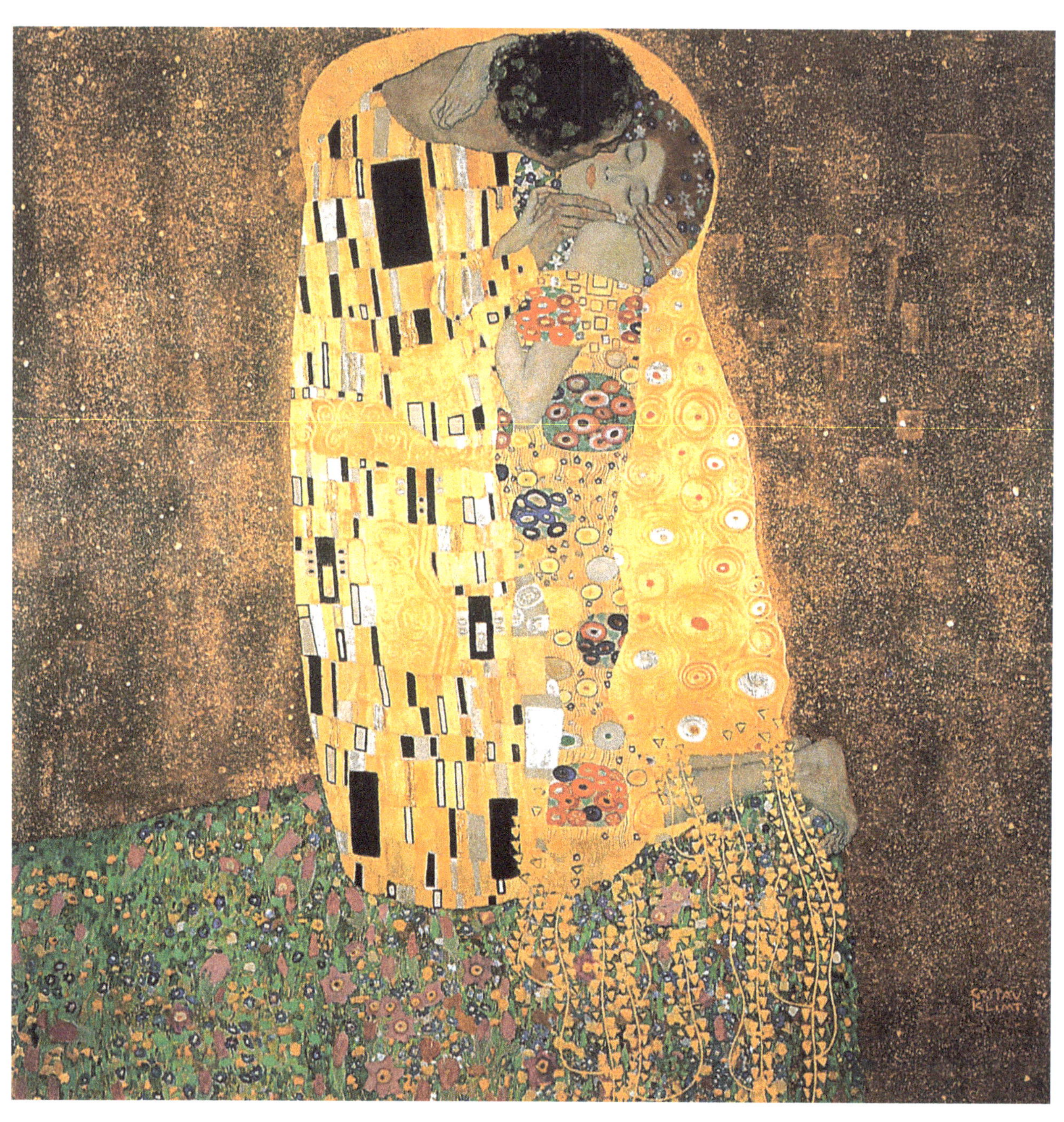

▲ **Gustav Klimt**, *The Kiss,* 1907-1908.
Oil, silver and gold on canvas, 180 x 180 cm. Österreichische Galerie Belvedere, Vienna.

ARTISTS OF THE VIENNESE SECESSION

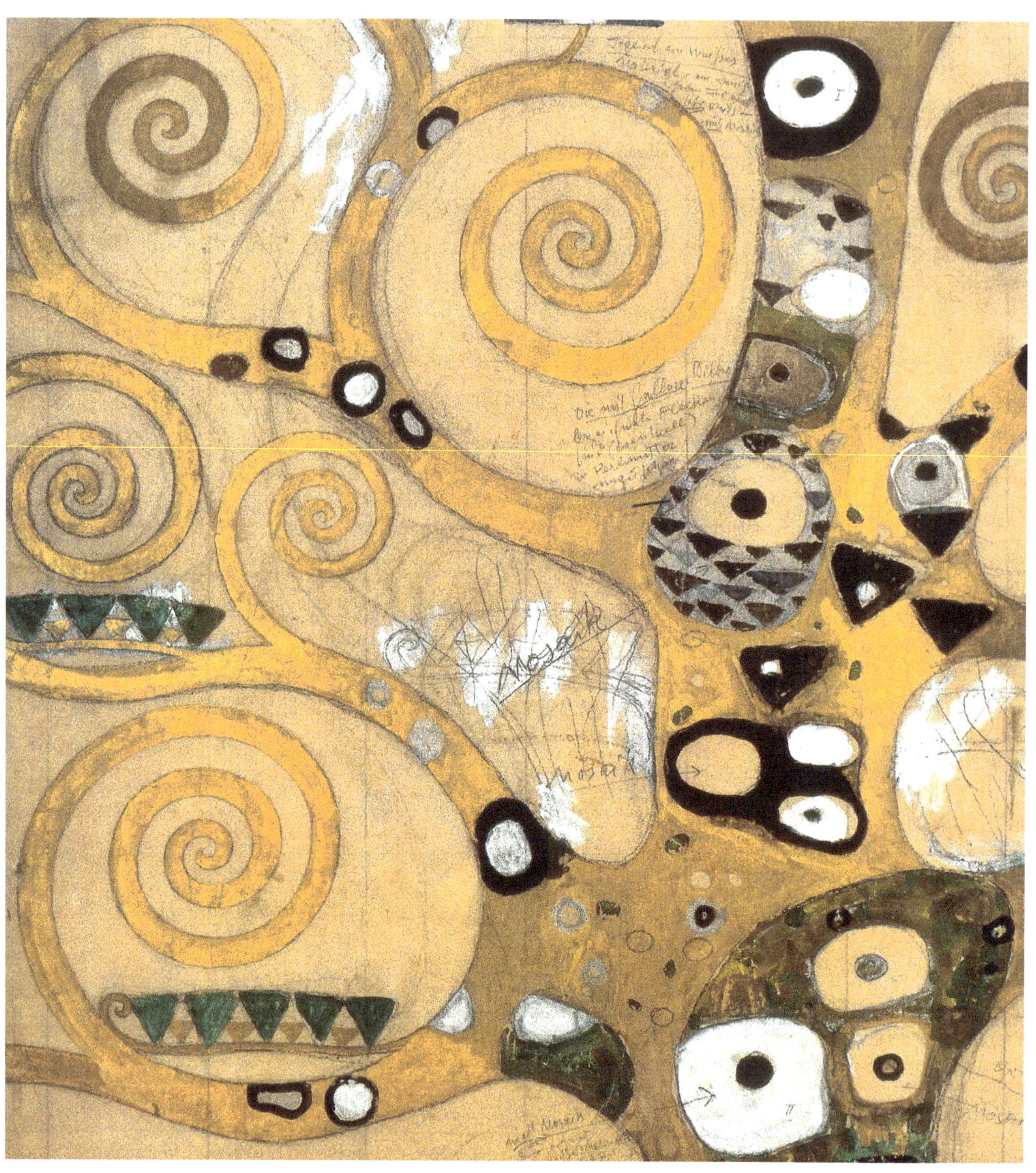

Gustav Klimt

(Baumgarten, 1862-1918, Vienna)

Gustav Klimt was the motor and the soul of the Viennese Secession, even though he had already left the Secession in 1905.

No connection to the outside world can disrupt the appeal of Klimt's portraits, landscapes, allegorical or other representative paintings. For the development of his seductive oeuvre, which has many aspects, one of them being a vehicle for the complete unravelling of the sensuality of the female body, Klimt makes use of oriental colours and motifs, a flat, two-dimensional canvas space, and strongly stylised images. Among his main inspirations were the art of Japan, ancient Egypt, and Byzantine Ravenna. He had already received a government allowance to study at Vienna's *Kunstgewerbeschule* (Artisan's School) as a 14-year-old teenager, where his talent as a painter and illustrator began to unfold. His first works therefore earned him an early and precocious success. His first important contribution to the world of art was the foundation of the artist group

◄ **Gustav Klimt**,
Tree of Life (detail), c.1905-1909.
MAK - Österreichisches Museum für Angewandte Kunst/
Gegenwartskunst, Vienna.

Künstler-Compagnie with his brother Ernst and friend Franz Matsch in 1879.

Late 19th century Vienna was in a period of architectonic transition since Kaiser Franz Joseph I decided to have the medieval city walls demolished in order to build the *Ring*. Since the areas surrounding the *Ring* were planned as upper-class residential areas, Klimt and his partners had many profitable opportunities to fill the walls of the new houses with art. In 1897, Klimt left the conservative *Künstlerhaus-Genossenschaft* (Artist's House Union) and founded the Secession along with a few close friends. Public acceptance of the movement soon followed.

The Secession did not only represent the very best in art that Austria had to offer, but it also helped to make Vienna an internationally recognised city of art by inviting foreign artists, like French impressionists or Belgian naturalists, to exhibit their work in the city. His rising fame as a modern artist in turn led to a decline of his reputation as an "acceptable artist" among the members of the Austrian upper class. The more he distanced himself from the academic style of his early artwork, the more he plunged into scandals surrounding his modern art. These scandals would direct his artistic career along new paths.

In 1894, Klimt and Matsch received the commission to create a wall painting for the festive hall of the Vienna University, which would include portrayals of the three most prominent courses of study – medicine, philosophy, and law. The nature of this commission is easily understood: the university expected a series of formal, dignified artworks in a classical style, which were supposed to portray the healing power of medical science, the wisdom of the philosopher, and undoubtedly the robed figure of Justice holding scales with blindfolded eyes representing law and jurisprudence. After a few years of hard work, however, the university received such a controversial painting that it immediately caused a scandal and sparked wild debates over its propriety. Klimt eventually had to pay back the advance and withdraw his paintings. Nevertheless, in 1900, Klimt received a golden medal for the painting *Philosophy* at the World Fair in Paris.

When he exhibited the unfinished painting *Medicine* in the following year, the outrage was even worse and the polemics reached an all-time high in their fervour. It is hard to say what Klimt wanted to express with this painting. The vision that the painting is conveying is chaotic and almost hellishly bleak. The skulls of old and wrinkled figures, and the randomly scattered people attest more to the decay and suffering of the human body rather than to its healing. The figure at the bottom with the snake wrapped around her arm is meant to represent the concept of medicine. Her portrayal, however, in her ornamental garment rather evokes the image of a priestess that is sacrificing the sick. The other female figure which is positioned beside the pillar of the human bodies and silhouettes is notable for her posture: her arms are thrown out as if mockingly imitating the crucifixion.

The sketch for this figure is a compelling proof of Klimt's extraordinary talent as an artist. The ductus of his pencil and the delicate shading lead our eyes to the pubic region of the woman. It is also interesting to note that the woman in the sketch is lying on the floor with her back pressed against an invisible object while she is standing unstably, unsupported as if she were to fall down every moment in the painting.

This work also represents a complete break with the tradition of depicting round and homely women that were predominant in the academic style of the nineteenth century. Klimt paints his women with long hair and lean, curvy bodies. Their sexual confidence makes them attractive but – in its directness – menacing at the same time. Klimt's contemporary, the journalist and critic Berta Zuckerkandl (1864-1945), noted in her memoirs:

> [...] Klimt transformed the Viennese women into the ideal type of woman: modern, with a boyish figure. These

Gustav Klimt, ▶
Medicine, 1900-1907.
Oil on canvas, 430 x 300 cm.
Burnt in 1945 at Immendorf Castle.

Gustav Klimt, ▼
The Beethoven Frieze (central panel, detail), 1902.
Casein on plaster, height: 220 cm.
Secession Hall, Vienna.

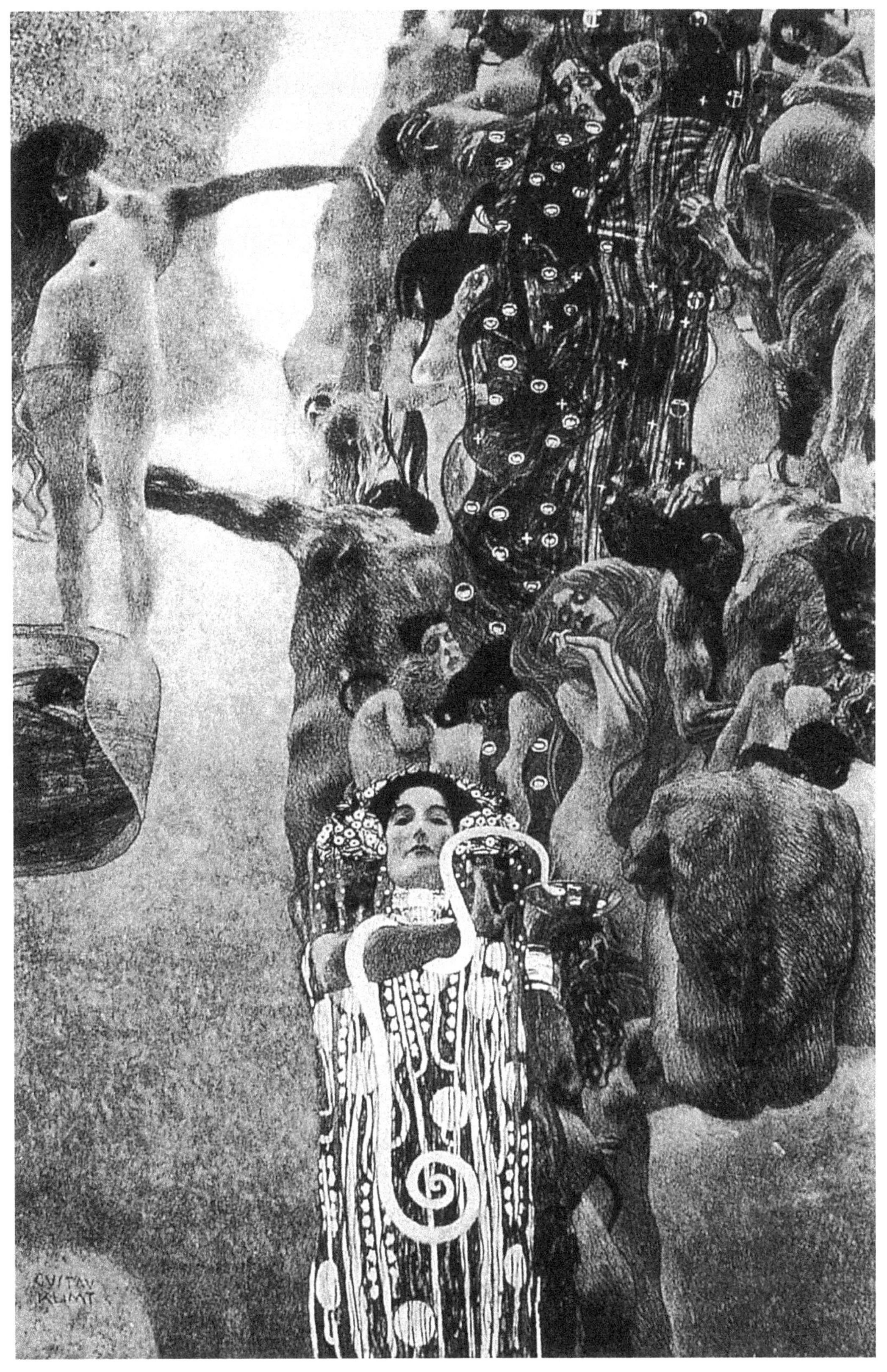

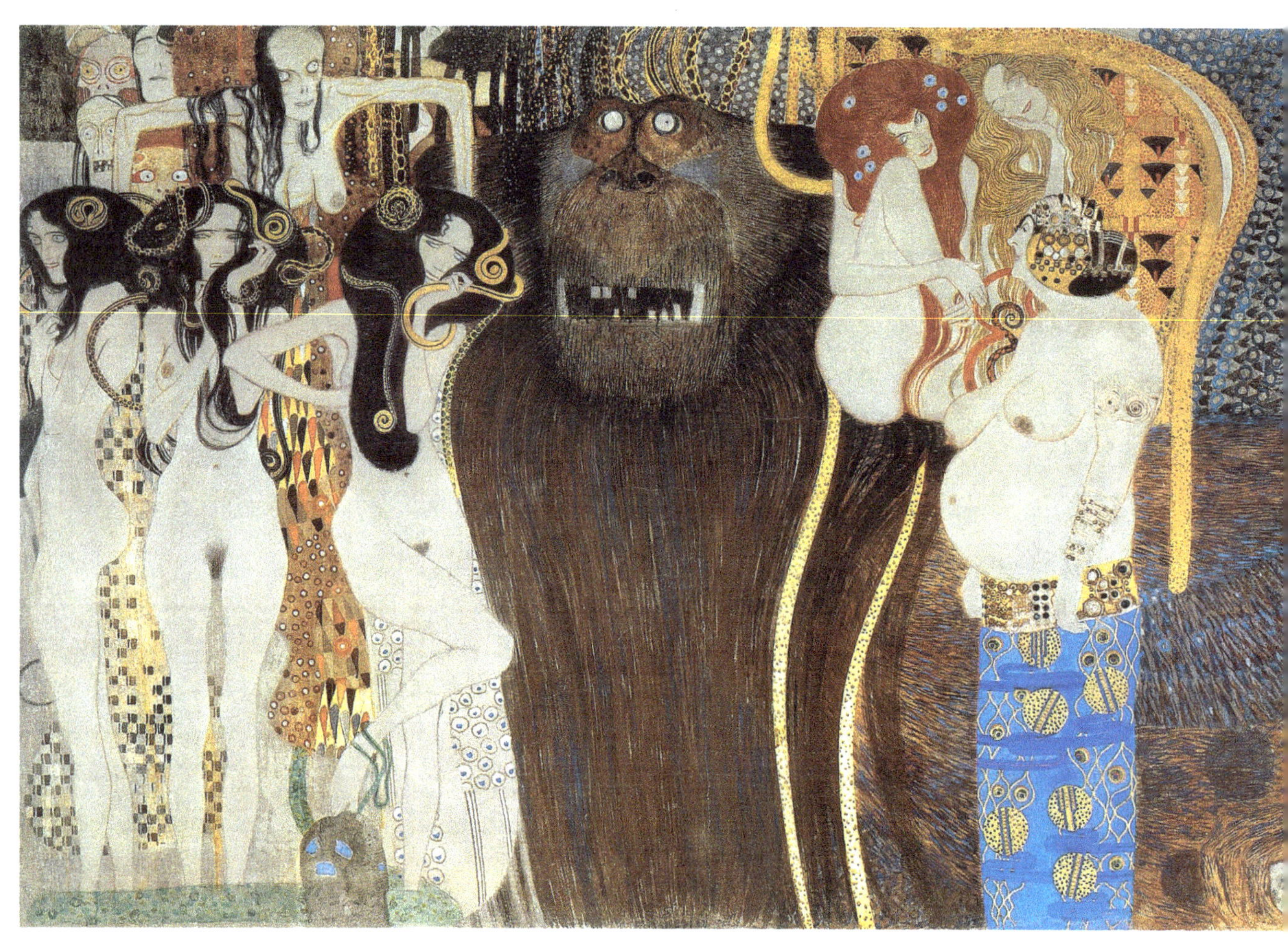

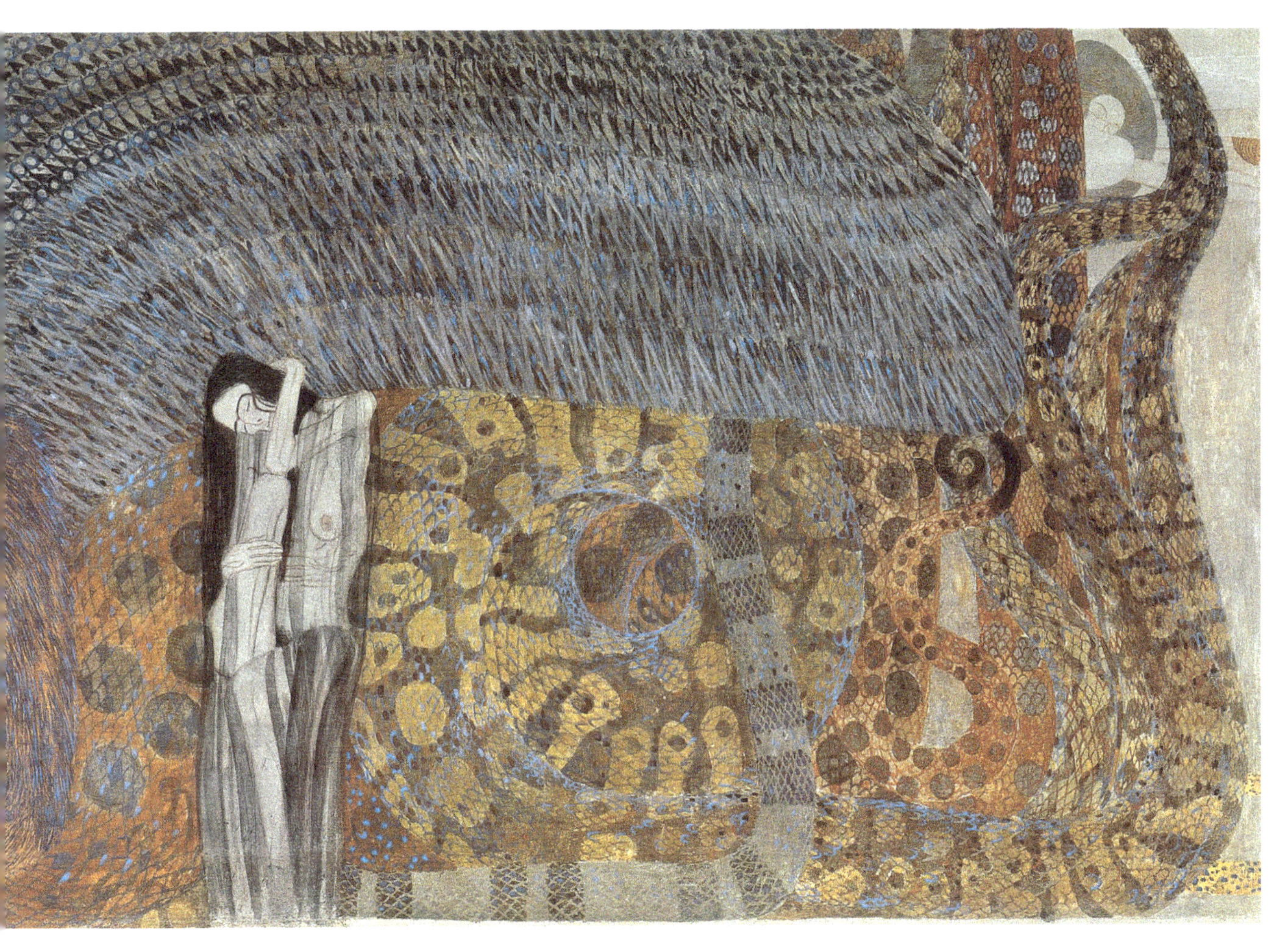

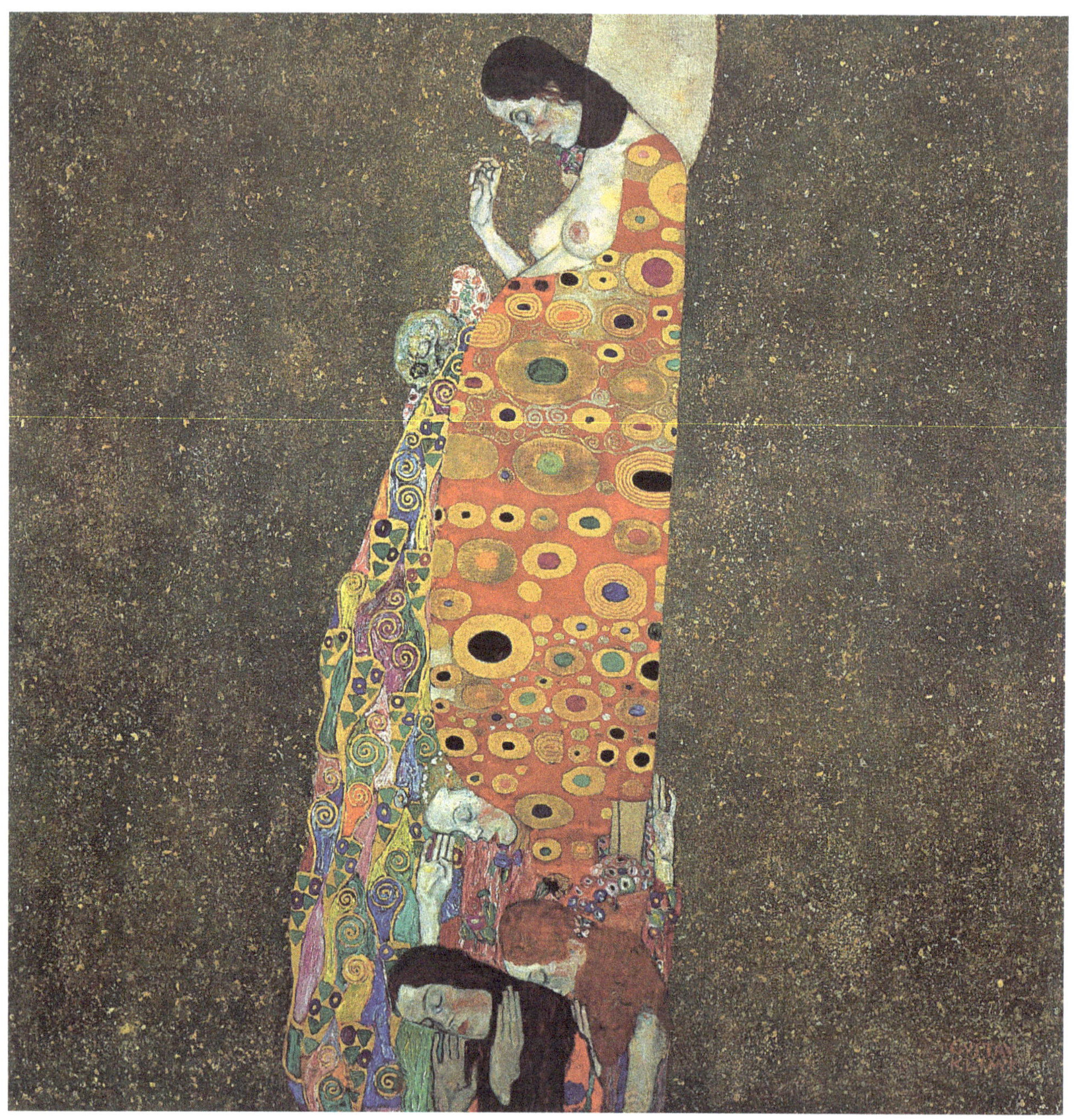

figures exerted a mysterious fascination on the viewer. Although the word "vamp" was not known back then, Klimt painted women who fit that description perfectly; women with the allure of Greta Garbo or Marlene Dietrich, long before they actually lived [...]

The 14th exhibition of the Secession in 1902, again, generated a hail of criticisms. The central object of the exhibition was Max Klinger's sculpture *Beethoven,* which Klimt sought to complement with a frieze that would be the backdrop for the exhibition room. One of the components of the frieze was a panel that showed three figures, *Lust, Gluttony,* and *Unchastity,* collectively called *Hostile Forces,* in Klimt's painting. Why Klimt chose his theme as a contribution to Beethoven of all things, was never entirely apparent. Nevertheless, this painting already showcases some of the Klimt-typical exotic ornamentation that would feature heavily in his later works. These ornaments were meant to create a composition in which decorative elements and the human figure can occupy the same space. In his portrayal of *Lust,* Klimt uses the figure's long hair to cover up her pubic region but, at the same time, also draws attention to it. The sumptuous depiction of *Gluttony* more resembles an oriental pasha than a woman – a man whose corpulence

◀ **Gustav Klimt**,
Hope II, 1907-1908.
Oil, gold and platinum on canvas, 110.5 x 110.5 cm.
The Museum of Modern Art, New York.

has reached the stage where his chest has transformed into huge breasts. Conservative Viennese society was deeply shocked by these paintings. A contemporary of Klimt once used the following anecdote:

> Suddenly the visitors of the exhibition could hear a scream from the middle of the room: "Ghastly!" A nobleman, customer, and art collector, whom, together with other close friends, the group had given early access to the rooms, lost his poise when faced with the frieze. He screamed the word with a high-pitched, shrill voice [...] He threw the word like a stone against a wall: "Ghastly!"

Klimt, who was standing on a scaffolding, working on his frieze just responded by throwing an amused look in the direction of the screaming man. This calm gesture best illustrates Klimt's usual reaction to the scandals that he caused. Although Klimt lost his imperial allowance due to the scandals surrounding the university paintings, as well as his support from the upper strata of society, he was still lucky enough to earn a sufficient amount of money through painting portraits. However, he was refused the chair for fine arts at the university more than once.

It is sometimes hard to realise that there are hardly any concrete details about the private life of a very famous man who lived not too long ago, compared with the information we have about the private lives of prominent figures from much more distant ages. The reason for this is Klimt's own discretion and reservedness. While many details illustrate his artistic career and are cemented by facts, the scarce information about his private life is based on accounts that are barely better than hearsay. On the one hand, he is portrayed as an insatiable womaniser with the physique of a peasant and the strength of an ox, who slept with numerous women, mainly his models. On the other hand, he seems like a hypochondriacal, self-confessed bachelor with routine habits, who lived with his mother and sisters and commuted daily to his studio in suburban Vienna.

Klimt never married but maintained a long-lasting relationship with the sister of his sister-in-law, Emilie Flöge. In 1891, his brother Ernst married Helene Flöge who ran a beauty salon together with her sister. The marriage only lasted 15 months but through Helene, Klimt was introduced to Emilie. From 1897 onwards, Klimt spent nearly every summer with the Flöge family in the village of Attersee. It was a calm and peaceful time for him which he used to paint the landscapes that account for almost a quarter of his oeuvre. The details of the relationship between Klimt and Emilie Flöge are sketchy, but several known facts still cause debates over how platonic their relationship really was. They never lived together but Klimt asked for Emilie's attendance at his deathbed. Throughout his life he maintained an extensive correspondence with Emilie and Marie Zimmermann, the mother of two of his three illegitimate children; his letters to Marie are affectionate, describing details of his work and life while letters to Emilie are rather bland and devoid of emotion just containing things like travel arrangements or travel descriptions.

The *Portrait of Emilie Flöge* shows an attractive young woman, who is wearing a dress of her own design as well as jewellery that was designed by Koloman Moser. Many of her dresses and fabrics were designed by Klimt specifically for her fashion salon. It is a remarkably defeating painting which is most notable for the delicate, almost poignant indication of sensuality that expresses itself in the smooth light on the skin above her bodice.

How different is this portrait with the painting *Hope I* (1903), which shows a nude pregnant woman, Herma, one of Klimt's favourite models. Supposedly, Klimt is reported to have said that her back was more beautiful and more intelligent than the faces of many other models. When she repeatedly failed to appear in his studio to model, Klimt, who was usually very concerned about his models, sent someone to enquire about her well-being. When he found out that she was not sick but pregnant he insisted that she come to his studio. Thus she became the model for *Hope I* and *Hope II*.

A remarkable example of Klimt's ability to use just a few pencil-drawn lines to create a sensual and erotic effect can be seen in the 1905/1906 sketch *Freundinnen in Umarmung* (*Friends in Embrace*). A small dark circle draws attention to the thighs and the buttocks of the woman. It is not uncommon for Klimt to draw his women while they are masturbating, revelling in their sensual pleasure with closed eyes

Gustav Klimt, ▶
Hope I, 1903.
Oil on canvas, 189.2 x 67 cm.
National Gallery of Canada, Ottawa.

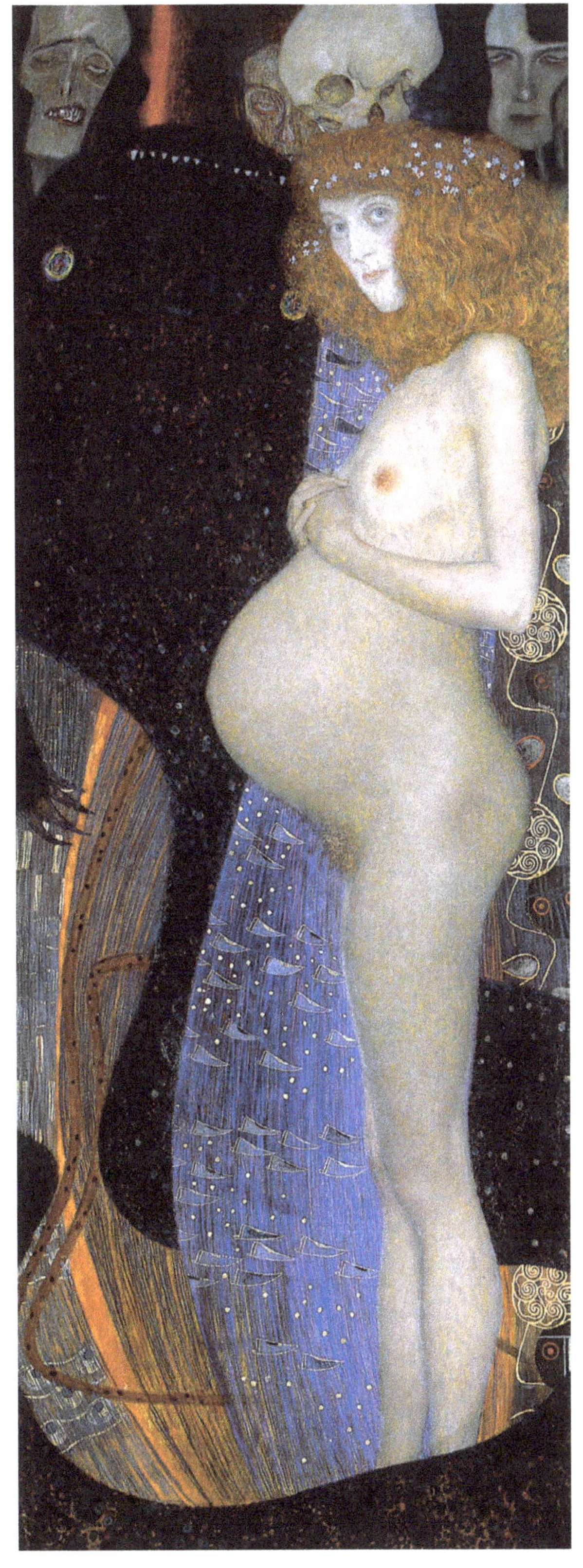

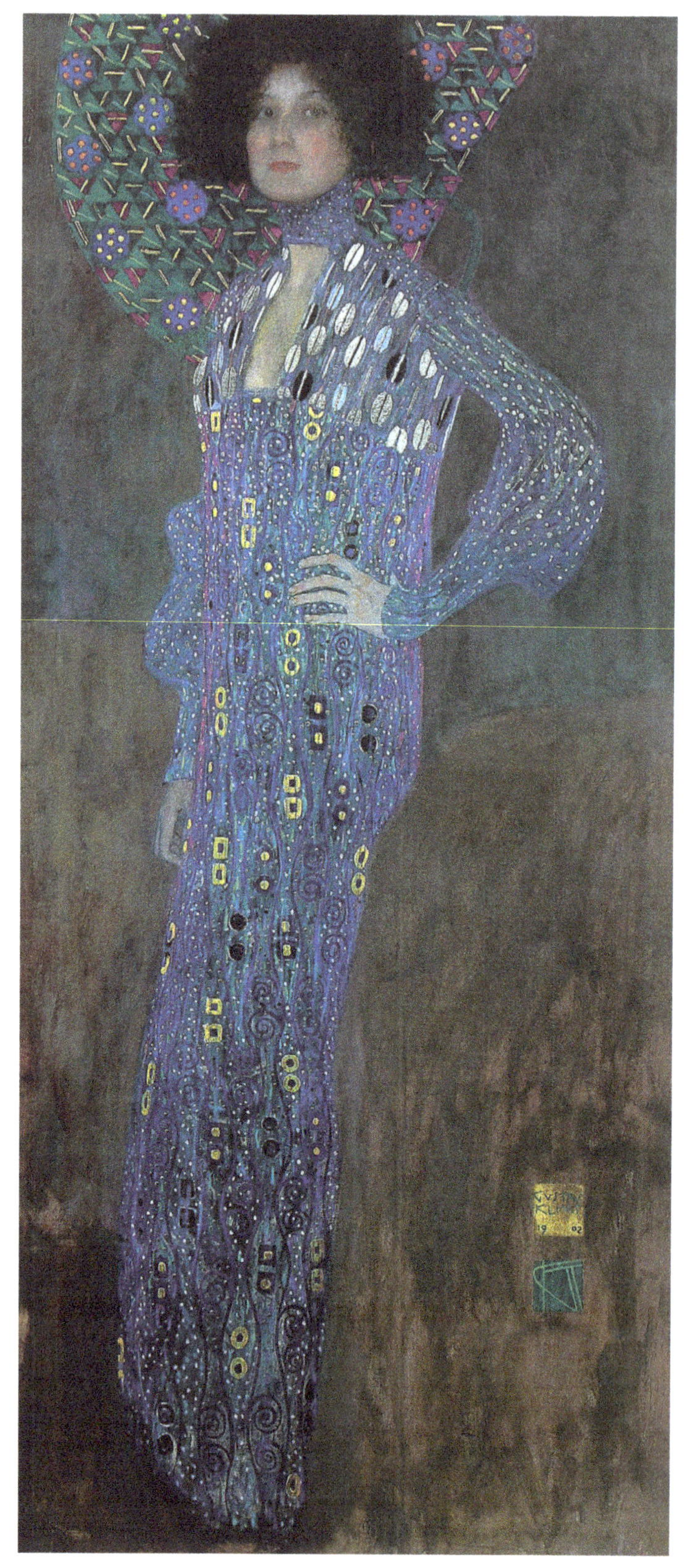

and face slightly averted. Men rarely appear in the pencil drawings; if they appear they are usually shown with their back towards the viewer.

While Klimt expresses his clear admiration for female beauty, he always shows a certain distance between the genders when he paints men and women together in a painting. In his most famous painting *The Kiss*, the face of the man is not visible, tellingly. He is holding the woman and his hands are cradling her face with great tenderness. Although she responds in kind, she still seems to shy away from the embrace. She just offers her cheek for the kiss and with her hands she seems to push away his.

The freedom in Klimt's drawings is a sharp contrast to the portraits of the ladies of fine society which he started painting in 1903. While the women in his drawings are not confined by clothing or society standards, the women in his portraits, like *Portrait of Fritza Riedler* or *Portrait of Adele Bloch-Bauer I*, are almost asphyxiated in fabrics and ornaments. Their faces are the focal points of the paintings while their bodies, in their ornamental dresses, almost fuse with the background. This allows the faces to appear almost fragile, detached and lonely. Another remarkable painting is the *Portrait of Margaret-Stonborough-Wittgenstein*, since it is one of the few images that is not dominated by patterned fabrics. Furthermore, it is a clear homage to James McNeill Whistler (1834-1903) whom Klimt greatly admired.

◄ **Gustav Klimt**,
Portrait of Emilie Flöge, 1902.
Oil on canvas, 181 x 84 cm.
Wien Museum Karlplatz, Vienna.

Throughout his whole life, Klimt only gave one comment about himself and his art:

> [...] I am convinced that I – as a person – am not extraordinary at all. I am simply an artist who is painting from morning to evening. I am not talented with words or letters, especially not when I have to talk about myself or my work. Only the idea of having to write a letter fills me with fear. I am afraid you have to make do without a portrait of myself, either painted or written. That is not a great loss, however. Whoever wants to get to know me better – as an artist only that is worth your trouble – should study my paintings and try to find out who I am and what I want [...].

Gustav Klimt was an unusual and highly extraordinary artist who had neither precursors nor successors. On 11 January 1918 he suffered a seizure which paralysed half his body. Despite a temporary recovery, he died a month later. After his death his reputation as an artist remained controversial. Art historian Hans Tietze (1880-1954), a friend of Klimt and author of his first monograph, describes his influence and legacy:

> [...] Klimt dragged Viennese art out of its isolation in which it had been rotting and opened up the world for it. At the turn of the century he was the guarantee, more than anyone else, for the artistic individuality of Vienna [...].

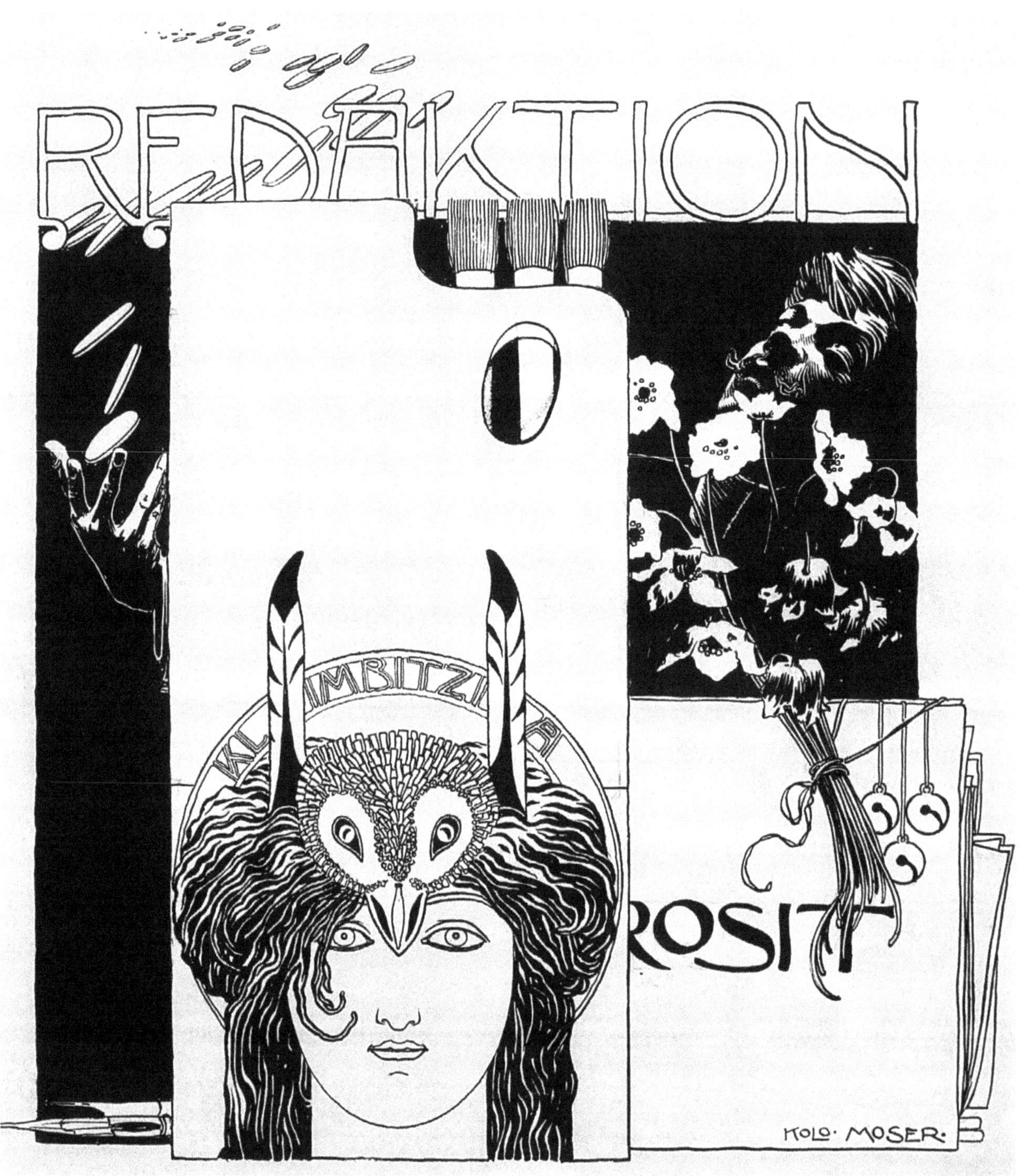
REDAKTION
KL...MBITZI...
ROSIT
KOLO· MOSER·

Koloman Moser

(Vienna, 1868-1918)

Koloman Moser was a pioneer of modernity. Not only was he the co-founder of the Wiener Werkstätte, but he also was the world's first graphic designer. He worked as a painter, illustrator, and artisan. Moser is also well known for his designs for jewellery, furniture, textiles and wallpapers. Before beginning his career as a multifaceted artist, Moser studied at the Academy of Fine Arts in Vienna where he was taught by Otto Wagner, the famous architect and city planner of Vienna and where he would later spend eight years teaching. He also attended courses by Franz Matsch and Gustav Klimt. During his studies Moser met the architects and decorators Joseph Maria Olbrich and Josef Hoffmann. His first work was a job as an illustrator for the art journal Meggendorfer Blatter

At the beginning of the 1890s, Moser began developing an innovative and highly individual variant of the *Jugendstil* while working as an illustrator. In 1897, he was part of the alliance of artists and architects surrounding Klimt, Olbrich, and Hoffmann, who founded the Secession to propagate radically new aesthetic ideas. Moser contributed heavily: he designed and also partly produced the stained glass windows, textiles, furniture, and different decorative objects for the Secession building. Furthermore, he created posters and illustrations.

During these years Moser was one of the most influential artists in Vienna. As an expression of his passion for *Jugendstil* he organised the sixth themed exhibition of the Secession. In the following years, he worked as a stage designer for the ensuing exhibitions of the group. In the same year, he began to create more and more monumental paintings which were especially remarkable for their bright colours. Moser's most important paintings were created in the second decade of the 20th century.

Moser also contributed to the magazine *Die Fläche* (*The Space*) and the self-styled "illustrated biweekly scripture for the artistic, spiritual and economic interests of urban culture" magazine *Hohe Warte;* both published in Vienna and Leipzig. Another title

◄ **Koloman Moser,**
Cover design for Meggendorfer Blätter (Meggendorf Folios), c. 1895.
China ink, collage on paper, 37.5 x 26 cm.
Collection and Archive, Universität für angewandte
Kunst, Vienna.

they used for their magazine was *Organ for the Nurture of Artistic Education*. Their topics included house-, city-, and interior architecture, but also with interior art, fine arts, and technology. The magazine staff represented the various fields of interests; among them architects Josef Hoffmann and *Jugendstil*-critic Hermann Muthesius (1861-1927). Later the group was complimented by another architect, the art theoretician Paul Schultze-Naumburg (1869-1949), who later joined the NSDAP and gathered questionable fame with his nationalistic art theory books *Kunst aus Blut und Boden* (*Art from Blood and Soil*) (1934) and *Rassengebundene Kunst* (*Race-Related Art*) (1934), and Professor Otto Wagner.

In 1903, Moser was involved in the foundation of another important association of artists, the *Wiener Werkstätte* (Vienna Workshops) which offered jobs and research opportunities to graduate students. They crafted the most diverse decorative objects in their studios: jewellery, tapestries, and articles of daily use. Some of these creations were used in the decoration of buildings that were conceived by the association-internal architects, like Otto Wagner.

In later years, Moser travelled and worked in different countries like France, Germany, Switzerland, and the Low Countries. He especially favoured the cities of Bern, Hamburg, and Paris. In 1905, he participated – together with Klimt and Josef Hoffmann – in the celebrated project of the now famous *Palais Stoclet* in Brussels. In the same year he left the Secession and two years later, also, the *Wiener Werkstätte*. His artistic style quickly started to change and transform, inspired by French and Belgian Art Nouveau, into a more sober version of the *Jugendstil* with long and geometrical shapes replacing the intricate and curved, endlessly dancing arcs.

Moser fused various influences from "high" art as well as from applied art, and was fascinated with the different branches of artistic expression, from painting to interior decoration and illustration. This makes him one of the artists who embodied the ideals of the *Jugendstil*, Art Nouveau, the Arts and Crafts Movement and ultimately the Secession. He died in October of 1918, aged 50, suffering from throat cancer.

Koloman Moser, ▼
Textile design "Abimelech" for Backhausen, design no 3806, 1899.
Pencil and watercolour on paper, 44 x 31 cm.
Backhausen Interior Textiles, Vienna.

Koloman Moser, ▼
Design for knotted carpet "Kleeblatt" (Shamrock) for Backhausen, design no 3436, 1898. Design for the Hotel Bristol in Bolzano.
Pencil and watercolour on paper, 48 x 60 cm.
Backhausen Interior Textiles, Vienna.

Koloman Moser, ▼
Design for furniture velour "Lindenblüten" (Linden blossom) for Backhausen, Design no 3732, 1899.
Design for the Hotel Bristol in Bolzano.
Pencil and watercolour on paper, 43 x 36.5 cm.
Backhausen Interior Textiles, Vienna.

Koloman Moser, ▼
Textile design "Vogel Bülow" (Golden oriole) for Backhausen, Design no 3600, 1899.
Pencil and watercolour on paper, 34 x 21 cm.
Backhausen Interior Textiles, Vienna.

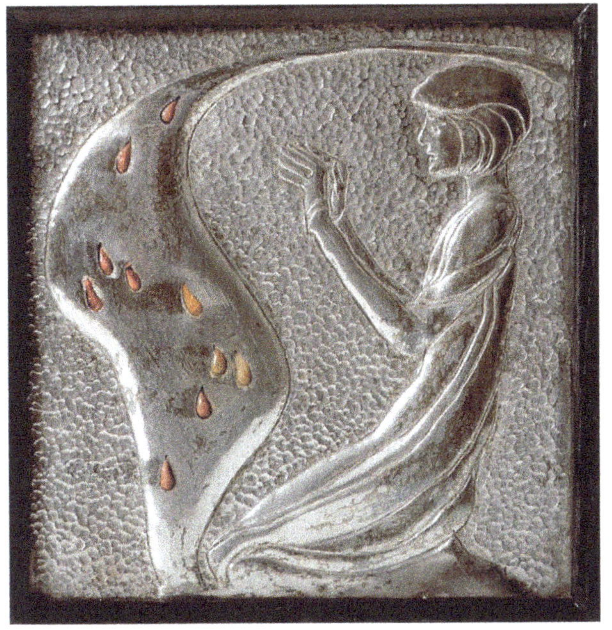 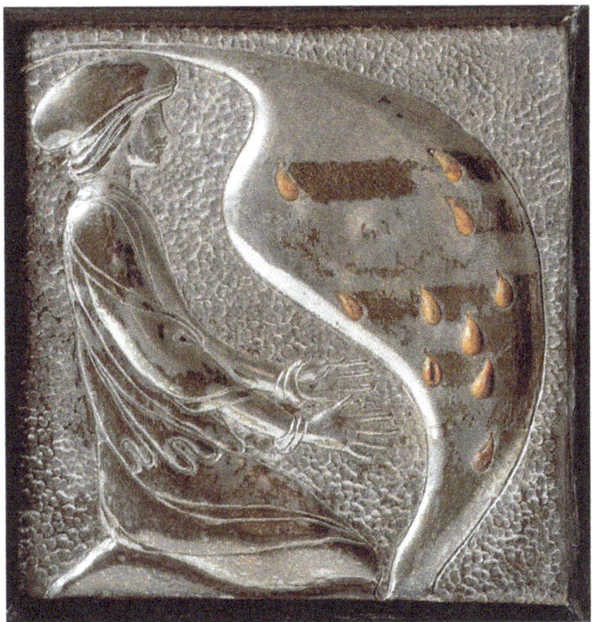

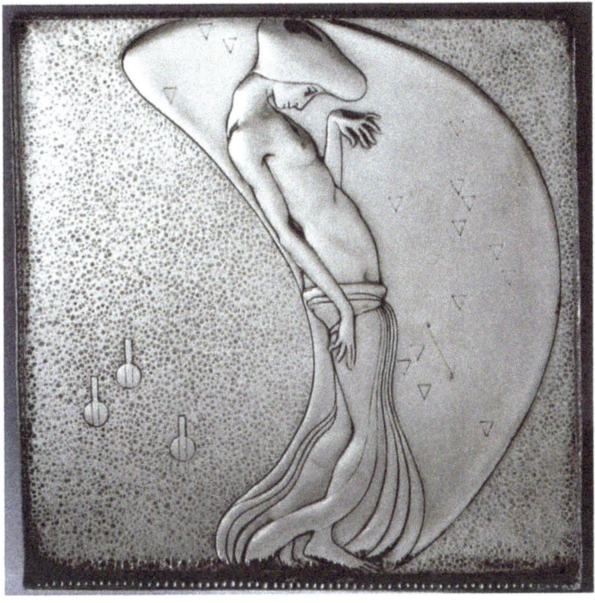 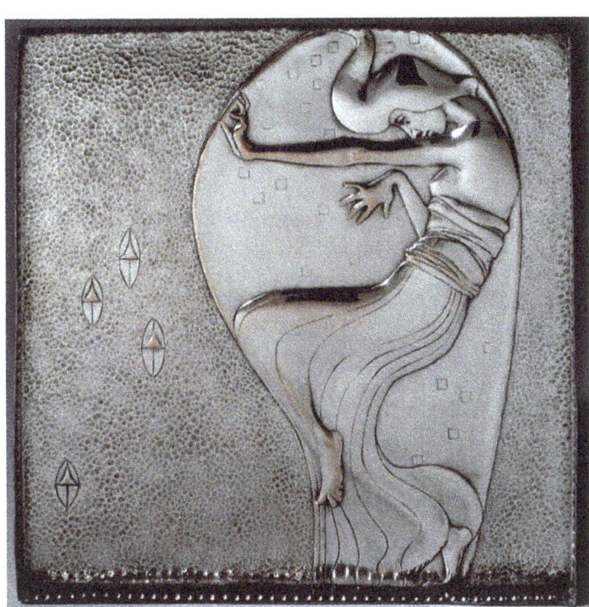

▲ **Koloman Moser**,
Metal reliefs for the offices of the *Wiener Werkstätte* in
Vienna VII, Neustiftgasse 32-34, 1904. Execution: *Wiener
Werkstätte* (Vienna Workshop).
Silver-plated copper, wooden frame, 15 x 14.8 cm each.
Wien Museum, Vienna.

▲ **Koloman Moser**,
Metal reliefs for a wall fitting in the drawing room of the
apartment of Dr. Hermann Wittgenstein, 1904.
Execution: *Wiener Werkstätte* (Vienna Workshop).
Silver-plated copper, 22.6 x 22.5 cm each.
Wien Museum, Vienna.

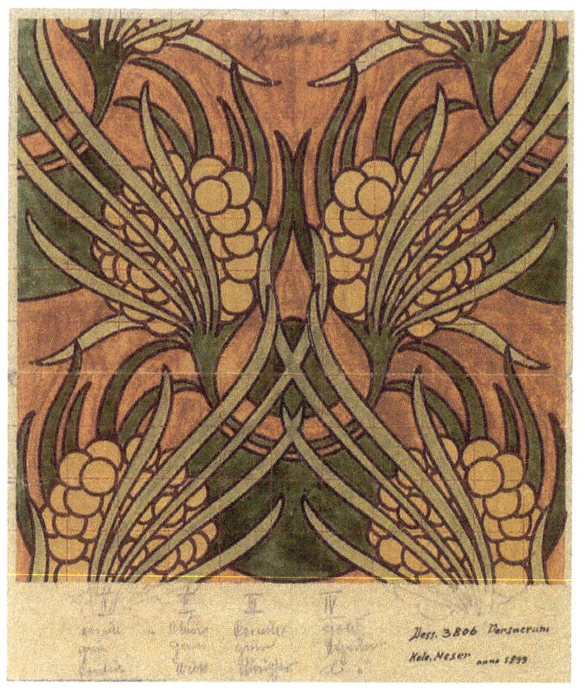

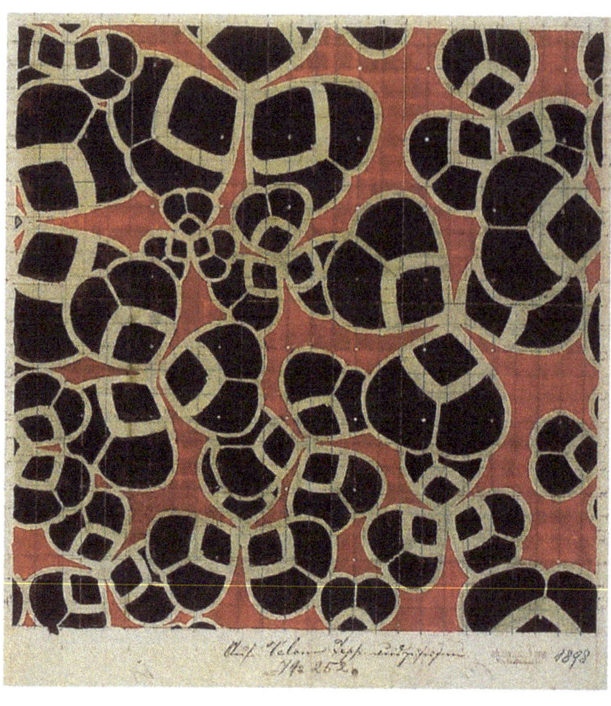

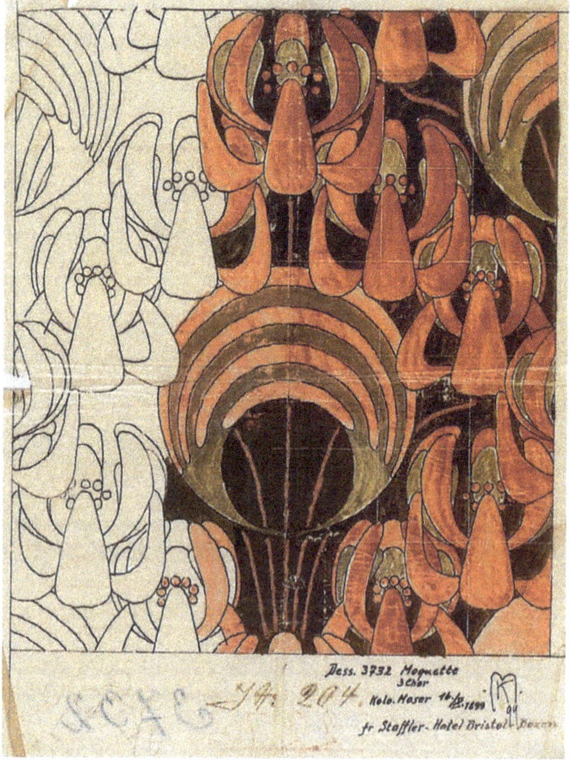

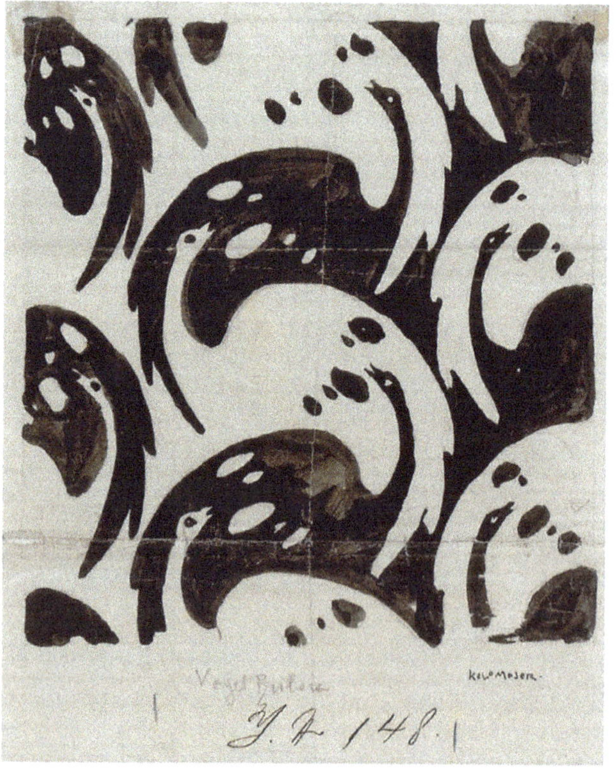

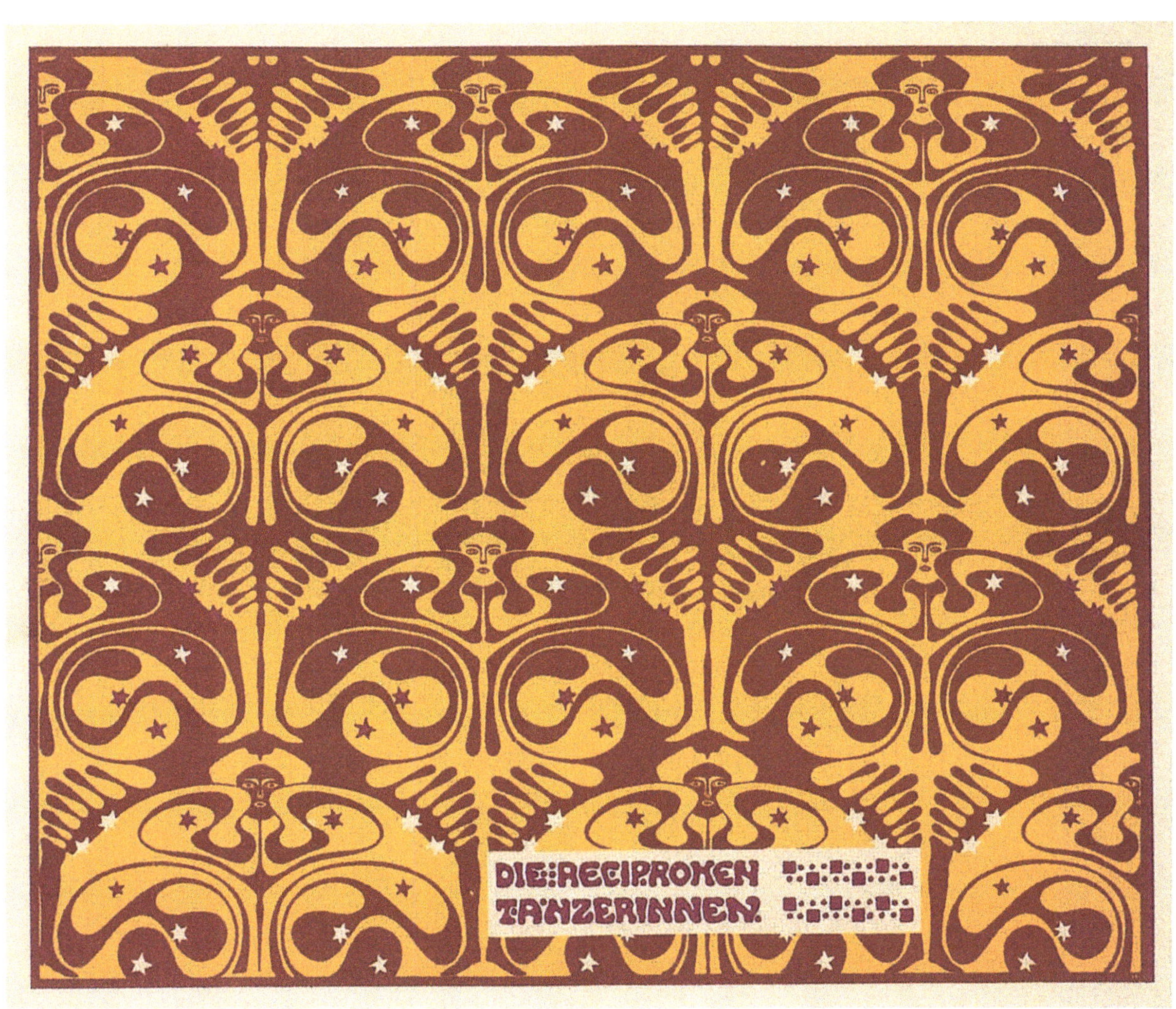

▲ **Koloman Moser**,
Die Reciproken Tänzerinnen (The Reciprocal Dancers), 1901.
Illustration in the portfolio *Die Quelle. Flächenschmuck von Koloman Moser,* (ed.) Martin Gerlach, published by Gerlach &
Schenk, Vienna, 1901. Coloured lithograph, 25 x 30 cm. Wien Museum, Vienna.

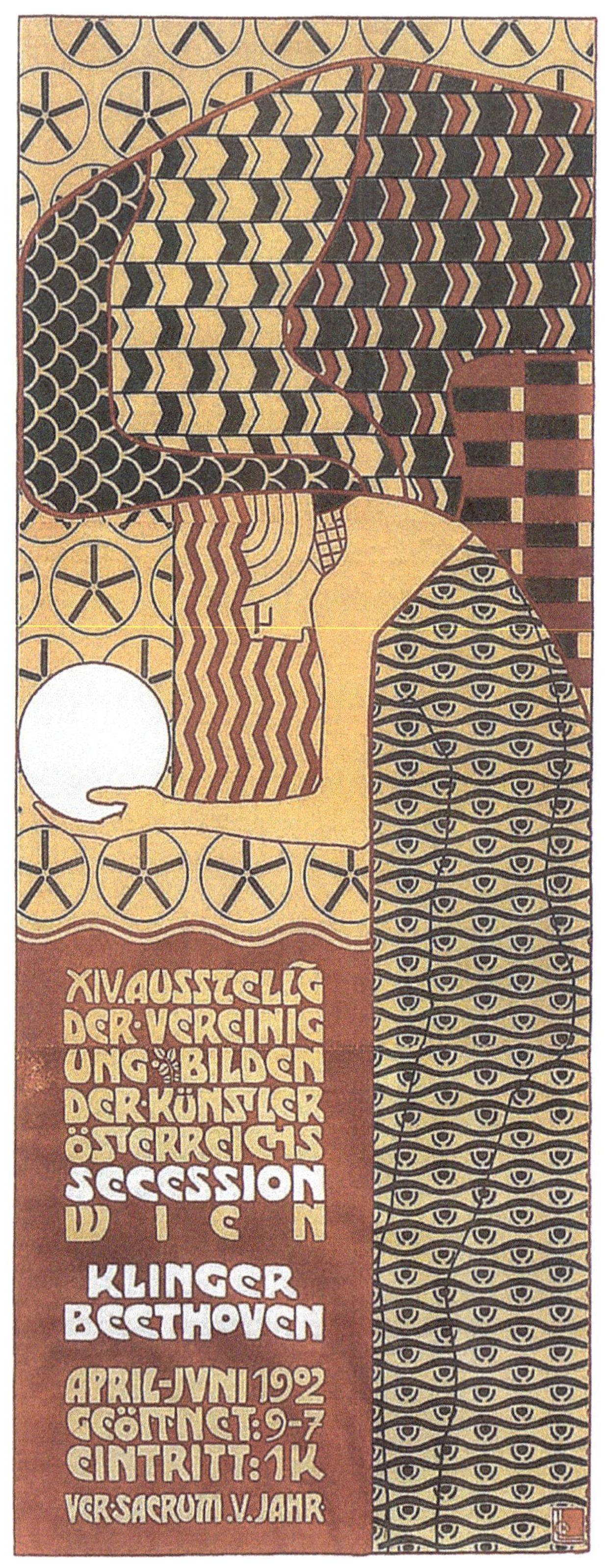

XIV·AUSSTELLG
DER·VEREINIG
UNG·BILDEN
DER·KÜNSTLER
ÖSTERREICHS
SECESSION
WIEN
KLINGER
BEETHOVEN
APRIL-JVNI 1902
GEÖFFNET: 9-7
EINTRITT: 1 K
VER·SACRVM·V·JAHR

Alfred Roller

(Brno, 1864-1935, Vienna)

Another founding member of the Viennese Secession who also acted as president from 1902 to 1905 was Alfred Roller, although he never attained the same fame as some of his colleagues. Today, he is mainly known in professional circles.

He took the main concept of his art, the idea of holistic art, from 19th century romantic Richard Wagner (1813-1883). Although Wagner was referring to the fusion of music and poetry, Roller adapted the concept for his own purposes and practiced it in his capacity as a stage designer. Prior to that, he designed the 1898 January cover of *Ver Sacrum*, developed several typefaces and posters for the 12th and the 14th exhibitions of the Secession. A photo, presumably from 1903, shows him together with Carl Moll, Gustav Mahler, and Max Reinhardt in the garden of Moll's villa, having a coffee break. Roller left the Secession in the same year as Klimt. Two years before that Gustav, Mahler had already invited him to work at the Vienna State Opera. After his departure from the Secession, it was his work at the State Opera that made him successful.

Aside from his friendship and working relationship with Mahler, he also collaborated with Richard Strauss (1864-1949). Roller designed and produced all stage settings for the debut performances of Strauss' plays. Later, he also worked at the *Burgtheater* (Imperial Court Theatre) with theatre director Max Reinhandt. Reinhardt also employed him as a teacher at his *Reinhardt-Seminar*, a workshop for actors. A whole generation of famous actors of the German-speaking parts of Europe graduated from the *Seminar*. Together with Reinhardt and Hugo von Hofmannsthal, Roller founded the Salzburg Festival as a successor to the late international music festivals. In collaboration with Hofmannsthal, he also created the stage design for Hofmannsthal's *Jedermann* (*Everyman*) (1911).

On a side note, a yet nameless admirer of Alfred Roller was a man named Adolf Hitler, who would have liked to start an apprenticeship with Roller. They presumably did not meet in Vienna but rather later when Hitler was already chancellor of the Reich and received Roller in an official capacity. Alfred Roller died on 21 June 1935 in Vienna.

◀ **Alfred Roller**,
Poster for the 14th Secession Exhibition:
Klinger, Beethoven, 1902.

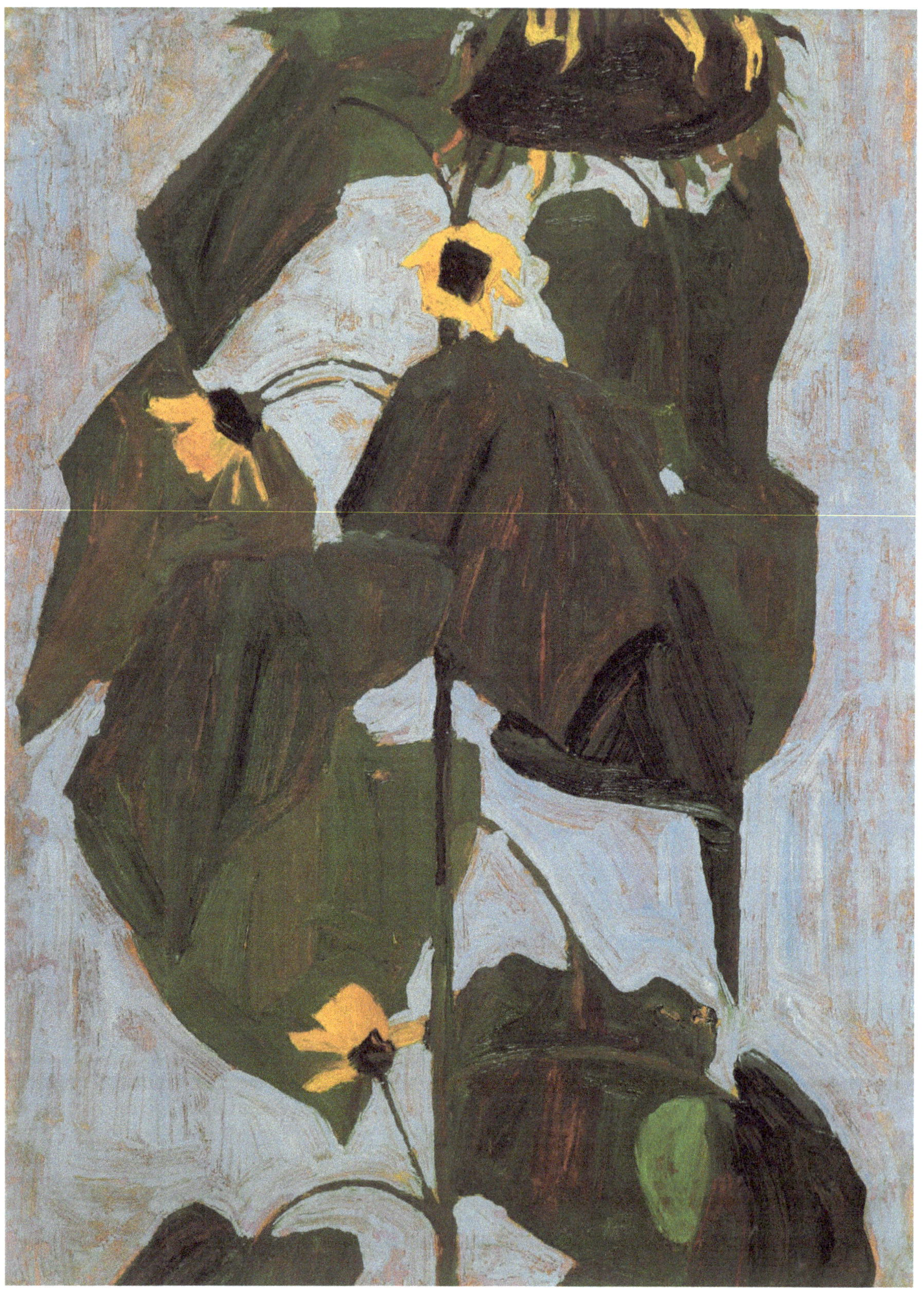

Egon Schiele

(Tulln, 1890-1918, Vienna)

Art cannot be modern, art is eternal.
Egon Schiele's oeuvre is unique to such an extent that it simply defies categorisation. Since he was initially heavily influenced by Gustav Klimt and the *Jugendstil*, he is also given space in this book, even though he later exhibited an art style that is closer to Expressionism than *Jugendstil*.

In modern industrial times, with the noise of racing steam engines, factories and the human masses working in them, Egon Schiele was born in the railway station hall of Tulln, a small, lower Austrian town on the Danube, on 12 June 1890. After his older sisters Melanie and Elvira, he was the third child of the railway director Adolf Eugen Schiele and his wife Marie (née Soukoup). The shadows of three male stillbirths were a precursor for the only boy, who in his third year of life would lose his ten-year-old sister Elvira. The high infant mortality rate was the lot of former times, a fate that Schiele's

◀ **Egon Schiele**,
Sunflower I, 1908.
Oil on cardboard, 44 x 33 cm.
Landesmuseum Niederösterreich, St. Pölten.

later work and his pictures of women would characterise.

In 1900, he attended the grammar school in Krems. But he was a poor pupil who constantly took refuge in his drawings, which his enraged father would burn. In 1902, Schiele's father sent his son to the regional grammar and upper secondary school in Klosterneuburg. The young Schiele had a difficult childhood marked by his father's ill health. He suffered from syphilis, which, according to family chronicles, he is said to have contracted while on his honeymoon as a result of a visit to a bordello in Triest. His wife fled from the bedroom during the wedding night and the marriage was only consummated on the fourth day, on which he infected her also. Despair characterised Schiele's father, who retired early and sat at home dressed in his service uniform in a state of mental confusion. In the summer of 1904, stricken by increasing paralysis, he tried to throw himself out of a window. He finally died after a long period of suffering on New Year's Day in 1905. The father, who during a fit of insanity burned all his railroad stocks, left his wife and children destitute. An uncle, Leopold Czihaczek, chief inspector of the imperial and royal railway, assumed joint custody of 15-year-old Egon, for whom he planned the traditional family role of railroad workers

.

During this time, young Schiele wore second-hand clothing handed down from his uncle and stiff white collars made from paper. It seems that Schiele had been very close to his father, for he, too, possessed a certain talent for drawing, collected butterflies and minerals, and was drawn to the natural world. Years later, Schiele wrote to his sister:

> [...] I have, in fact, experienced a beautiful spiritual occurrence today, I was awake, yet spellbound by a ghost who presented himself to me in a dream before waking, so long as he spoke with me, I was rigid and speechless.

Unable to accept the death of his father, Schiele let him rise again in visions. He reported that his father had been with him and spoken to him at length. In contrast, distance and misunderstanding characterised his relationship with his mother who, living in dire financial straits, expected her son to support her; instead, the eldest sister would work for the railroad. However, Schiele, who had been pampered by women in his childhood, claimed to be "an eternal child". By a stroke of fate, painter Karl Ludwig Strauch (1875-1959) instructed the gifted youth in draughtsmanship; the artist Max Kahrer of Klosterneuburg looked after the boy as well. In 1906, at the age of only sixteen, Schiele passed the entrance examination for the general art class at the Academy of Visual Arts in Vienna

on his first attempt. Even his strict uncle, in whose household Schiele now took his midday meals, sent a telegram to Schiele's mother: "Passed".

His sister, four years his junior, was a compliant subject for him. The nude study of the fiery redhead with the small belly, fleshy bosom and tousled pubic hair is his younger sister Gertrude (1894-1981). In another watercolour, Gerti reclines backwards, still fully clothed with black stockings and shoes, and lifts the black hem of her dress from under which the red orifice of her body appears. Schiele draws no bed, no chair, only the provocative gesture of his sister's body offering itself (*Reclining Girl in a Dark Blue Dress*, c. 143).

At the same time as Sigmund Freud was postulating that self-discovery occurs by means of erotic experiences, and "the urge to look" emerges as a spontaneous sexual expression within the child, young Egon recorded confrontations with the opposite sex on paper. He incorporated erotic games of discovery and an unabashed interest in the genitalia of his model into his nude studies; the forbidden gaze, searching for the opened female vagina beneath the rustling of the skirt hem and white lace. Gerti, with her freckled skin, green eyes, and red hair, is the prototype of all the later women and models of Schiele.

Egon Schiele, ▶
Portrait of Gerti Schiele, 1909.
Oil, silver, gold-bronze paint and pencil on canvas,
139.5 x 140.5 cm.
The Museum of Modern Art, New York.

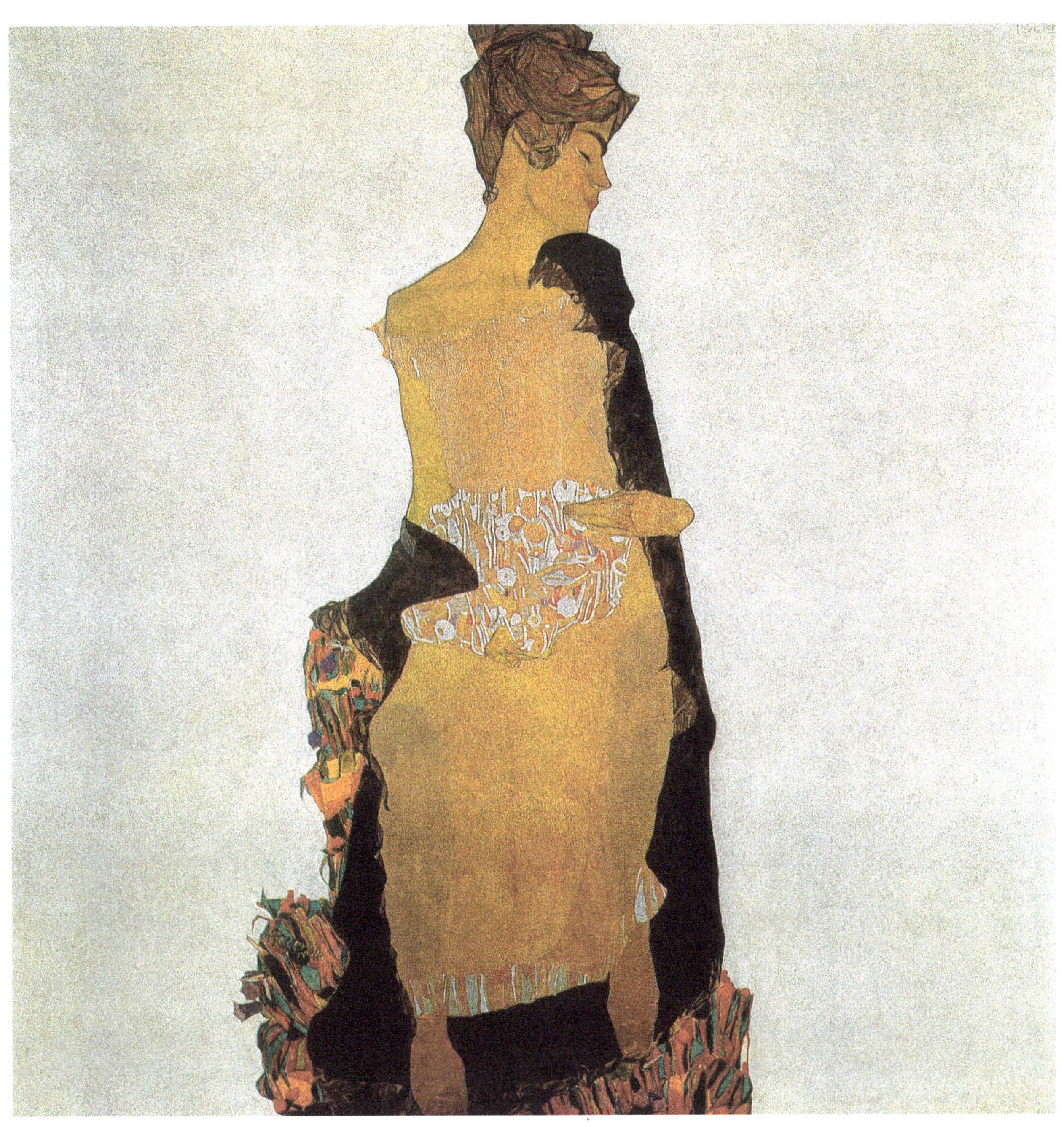

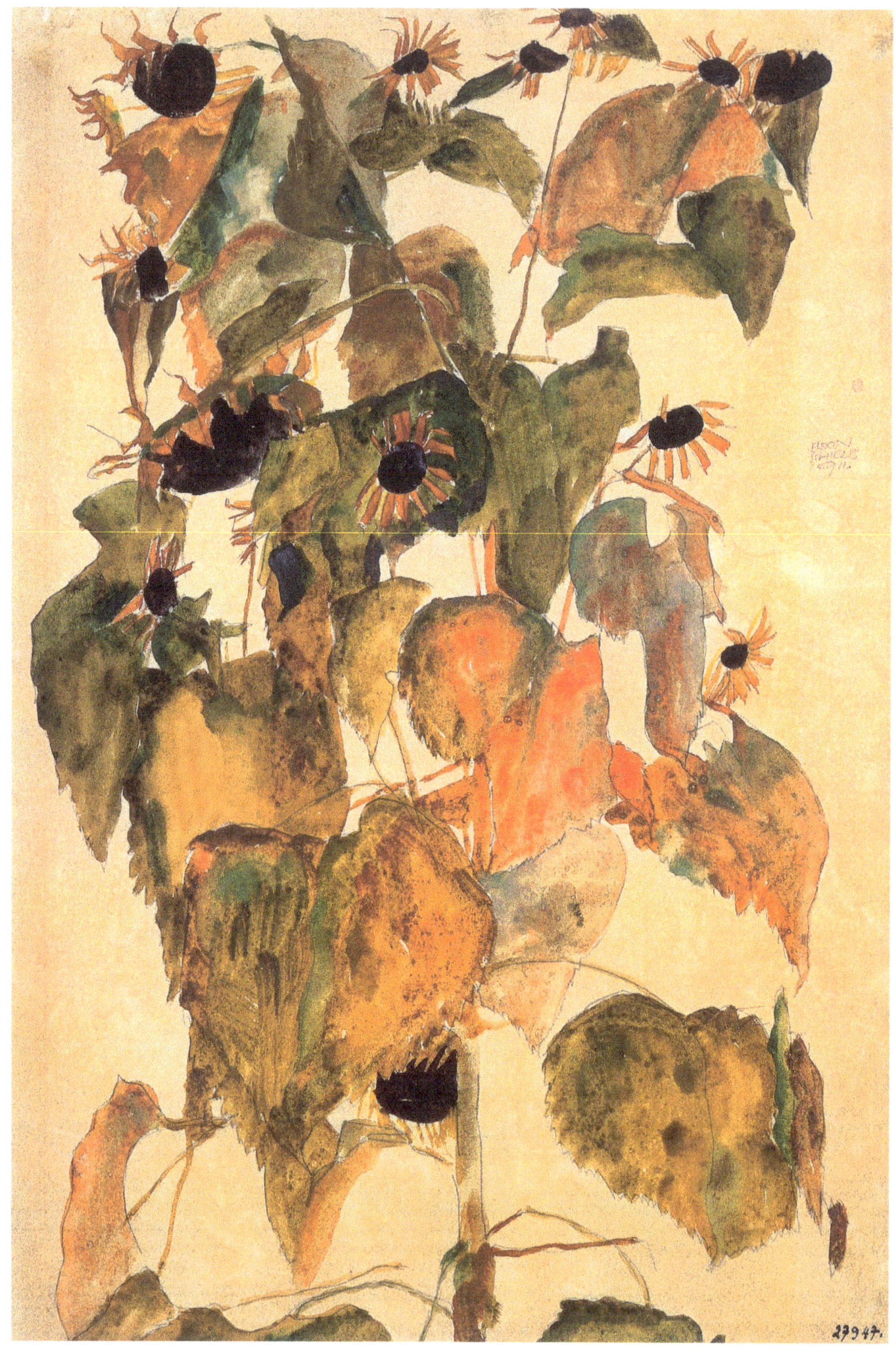

Schiele's roots can be found in the *Jugendstil* of the Viennese Secession. Like many other artists who joined the movement, he followed the famous and charismatic Gustav Klimt. Schiele met Klimt in 1907 and they immediately befriended each other. Klimt even modelled for one of Schiele's sketches. Schiele played to his strength by employing his exceptional skill in manipulating the composition and thus creating works with a tense expressiveness. He was deeply convinced of his own artistic importance and thus achieved more in his short life than many other artists have in a long one.

Schiele slowly veered away from *Jugendstil* and more towards Expressionism. This is most obvious when comparing Klimt's *Kiss* with any painting that his former protégé created at the same time. Klimt's painting was exhibited in 1908 as the central piece in a special hall of the *Kunstschau* (Art Show) which also displayed another 16 of his more recent paintings. *The Kiss* was the culmination of a development that had begun with two opulent wall paintings, the *Beethoven Frieze* from 1902 and the wall mosaics which he created between 1905 and 1909 as decoration for the dining room of Josef Hofmann's *Palais Stoclet* in Brussels.

Although the painting was already regarded as a sumptuous icon of sensuality, it was still not decorative enough to be bought by the government. The painting shows a magical, ethereal dreamscape in which a man is embracing a woman who seems to fall unconscious at the touch of lips. They are surrounded by glimmering gold, silver and minute blossoms. The "biomorphic" shape of the halo-like aura which surrounds the couple alludes to the blossoming of sexual passion and serves the religious function of an altar at the same time. Klimt himself did not bother to hide the subtle eroticism of his painting. Some of his friends (including Schiele) explained that the broad back of the man is not only representative of his potency but is also supposed to look like the underside of a phallus.

Unlike Klimt, Schiele found his models on the streets: young girls of the proletariat and prostitutes; he preferred the child-woman androgynous types. The thin, gaunt bodies of his models characterised lower-class status, while the full-bosomed, luscious ladies of the bourgeoisie expressed their class through well-fed corpulence. Yet, the attitude of the legendary Empress "Sissi" is symptomatic of a time in which the conventional image of women began to change. She indeed bore the desired offspring; however, she rebelled against the maternal role expected of her. The ideal of a youthful figure nearly caused her to become anorexic. At the same time, she shocked Viennese court society not only with her unconventional riding excursions, but also in that she wore her clothing without the prescribed stockings.

Around the time of the *fin de siècle*, Schiele portrayed young working-class girls. The number

◄ **Egon Schiele**,
Sunflowers, 1911.
Pencil and watercolour on paper, 44.5 x 30.5 cm.
Albertina, Vienna.

of prostitutes in Vienna was among the highest per capita of any European city. Working-class women were where upper-class gentlemen found the defenceless objects of their desire, which they did not find in their own wives. The young, gaunt bodies in Schiele's nude drawings almost stir pity; red blotches cover their thin skin and skeleton-like hands. Their bodies are tensed; however, the red genitalia are full and voracious. Like little animals, they lie in wait for the lustful gaze of the beholder. Despite their young age, Schiele's models are aware of their own erotic radiance and know how to skilfully pose. The masturbating gesture of the hand on the vagina accompanies the provocative gaze of the model. Contrary to the hygienic taboos of the upper class, for example, not to linger overly long while washing the lower body and not to allow oneself to be viewed in the nude, Schiele's drawings testify to a simple body consciousness and a matter-of-fact attitude. For the lower levels of society, "love for sale" pertained to earning one's daily bread.

Schiele's productive life scarcely extended beyond ten years, yet during this time he produced 334 oil paintings and 2,503 drawings (according to Jane Kallir, New York. 1990). He painted portraits and still-lifes, as well as land and townscapes. However, he became truly famous for his draughtsmanship. Even his most scant sketches are the result of his extraordinary skill of observation. Similar to many other artists of his age, he deeply analyses his inner life and his subjects. According to expressionist ideas this first introspective step is what truly defines the artistic process of creation.

While Sigmund Freud exposed the repressed pleasure principles of upper-class Viennese society, which put its women into corsets and bulging gowns and delegated them a static and lone role as future mothers, Schiele bares his models. His nude studies penetrate brutally into the privacy of his models and finally confront the viewer with his or her own sexuality.

The photograph of Schiele on his deathbed depicts the 28-year-old looking asleep, his gaunt body completely emaciated, his head resting on his bent arm; the similarity to his drawings is astounding. Because of the danger of infection, his last visitors were able to communicate with the Spanish flu-infected Schiele only by way of a mirror, which was set up on the threshold between his room and the parlour.

On October 31, three days after the death of his wife who was six months pregnant, Schiele also died from Spanish flu. Three days later, on 3 November 1918, the Austro-Hungarian Empire capitulated. Earlier in the same year, 1918, Schiele designed a mausoleum for himself and his wife. Did he know, he who had so often distinguished himself as a person of foresight, of his impending death?

Egon Schiele, ▶
The Dancer Moa, 1911.
Pencil, watercolour and gouache on paper, 47.8 x 31.5 cm.
Leopold Museum, Vienna.

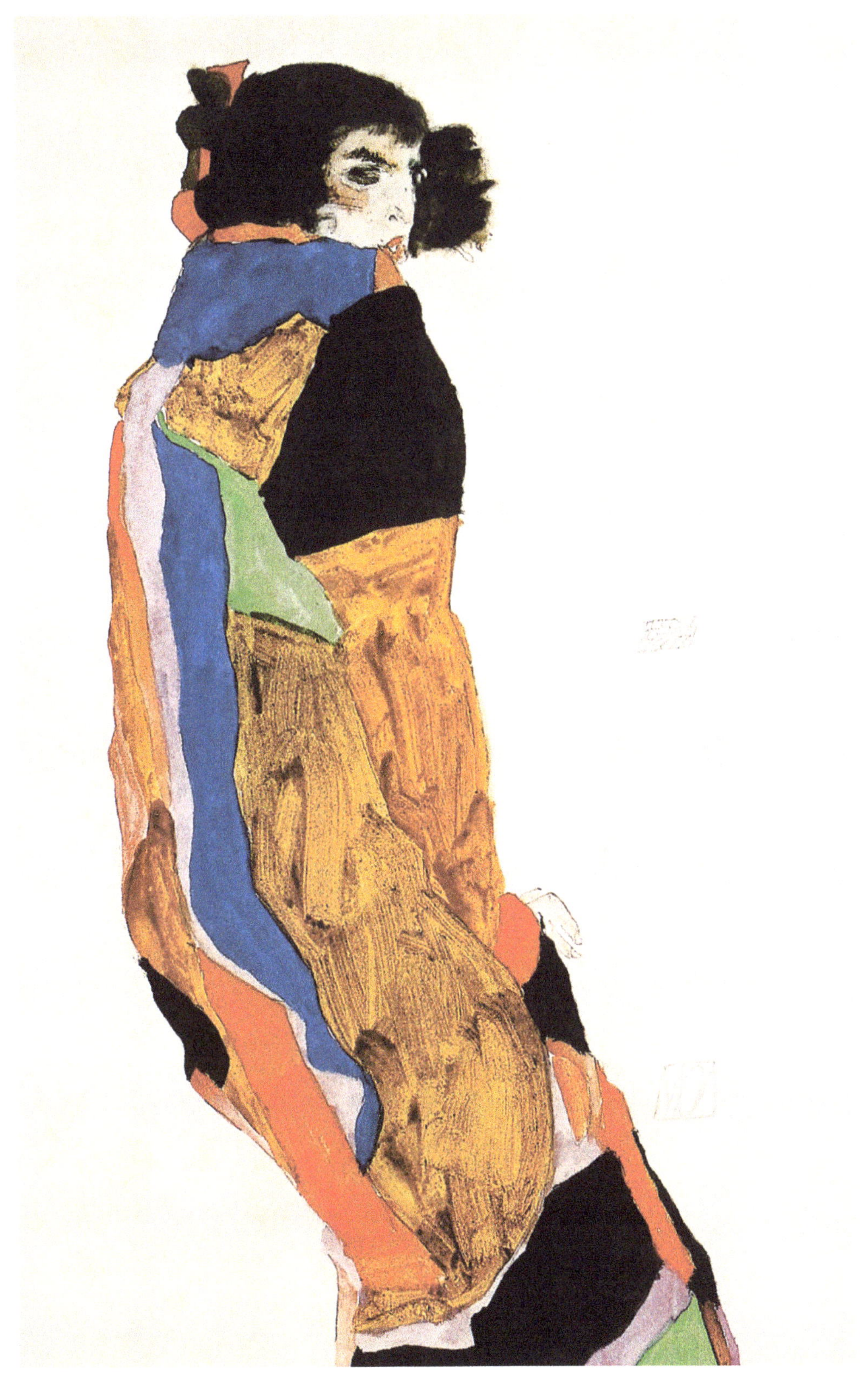

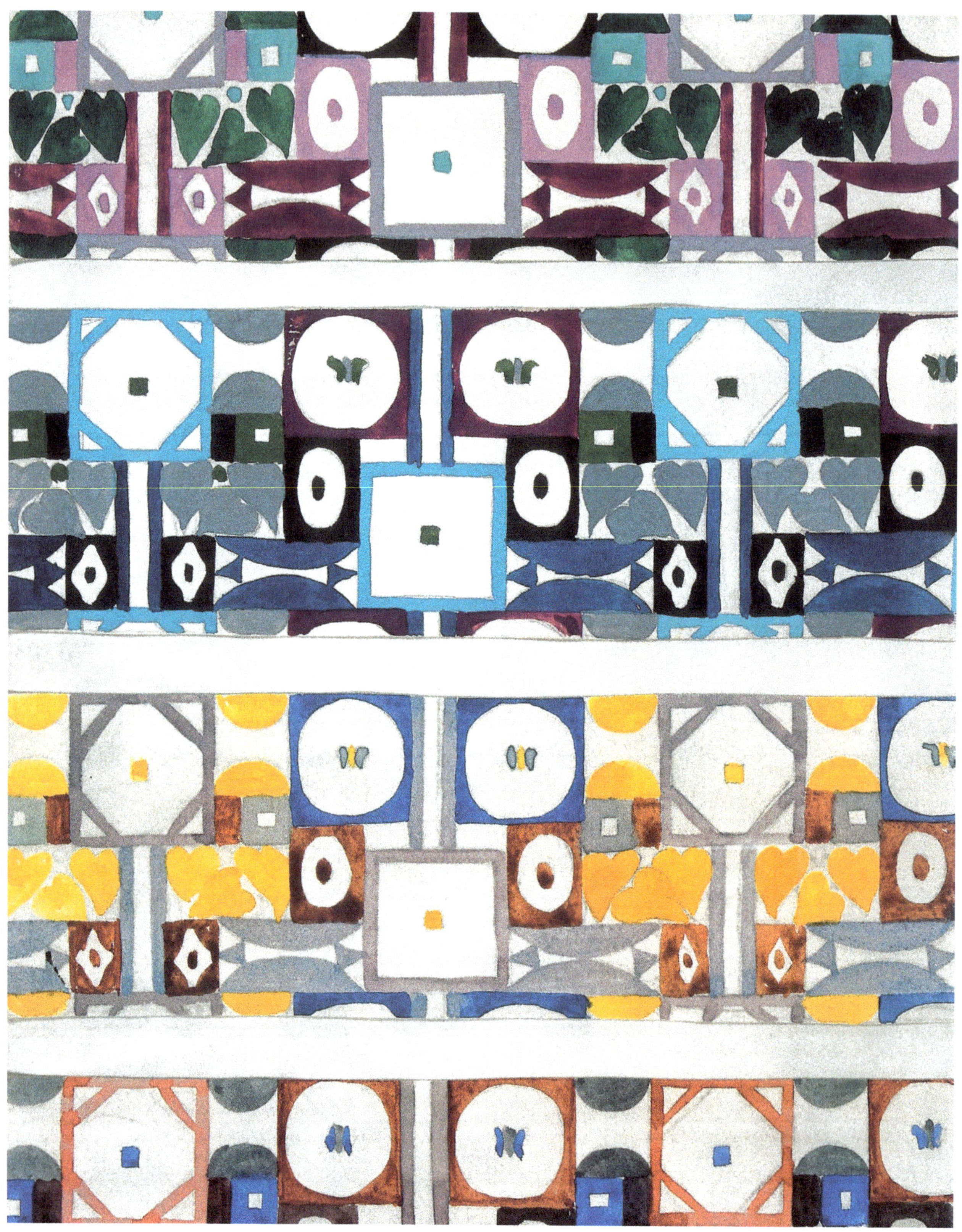

WIENER WERKSTÄTTE

A few members of the Viennese Secession had been contemplating the current condition of Austrian craftwork for years and found it severely lacking in many areas. In 1903, these artists decided to form the *Wiener Werkstätte*, a so-called *Produktiv-Gemeinschaft von Kunsthandwerkern in Wien* (Productive Community of Artisans in Vienna), which would last until 1932. They were essentially following in the footsteps of a development that had begun with the 19th-century *Arts and Crafts Movement* in England. The movement experienced its zenith between 1880 and 1920 and was most influenced by the painter, architect, and artisan William Morris and the art historian John Ruskin. In Germany, a similarly minded development resulted in the foundation of the *Deutscher Werkund* and later, the *Bauhaus*.

Ludwig Hevesi enthusiastically welcomed the event in an article from 21 January 1905:

◀ **Josef Hoffmann**,
Fabric design: Kiebitz, 1910-1915.
Wiener Werkstätte (Vienna Workshop). no 365.

[...] Today, *Der Kunstwanderer* presents as a novelty in this year's series, the *Wiener Werkstätte*. This unusual but laudable undertaking is one of the most joyous developments in Vienna's modern craftwork scene. It is especially remarkable since this project was set in motion by private citizens basing their decision on the righteousness and common sense of their own principles. We are facing a successful initiative of pragmatic idealists which no one would have dared to attempt to start a few years ago.

In secrecy, without the noisiness that is supposedly typical of craftwork, an artistic focal point has been created that is focused on reasonable, aesthetic and especially honest work with various materials. The principle of honesty that has been the mark of this new group from the very beginning, had nearly been lost in the current age of the machine and European-American mass production (according to the motto "cheap and bad").

The desire for honesty in the applied arts was ultimately the catalyst for the change. The *Wiener Werkstätte* is today – and we want to say "hopefully" – just a beautiful beginning. It bears the seed for a healthy school for artisanship and artisans and thus also for the consuming public [...].

Josef Hoffmann took on the artistic direction of the *Wiener Werkstätte*. As professor for architecture at the *Kunstgewerbeschule*, he had already worked with Koloman Moser before their *Werkstätte*-co-operation. They were joined by Fritz Waerndorfer, an industrialist and patron of the arts who volunteered to attend to the financial details of the venture, since artists were said not to have a very good comprehension of commercial issues back then; it was Hermann Bahr who introduced the two artists to Waerndorfer.

In an incredibly short amount of time, the *Werkstätte*, with their array of products ranging from Olbrich's cutlery and *Jugendstil*-posters to complete furnishings for residential houses, were successful to such a degree that they had to hire a hundred more employees in order to handle the rising demand. Furthermore, they could open branches in Karlsbad, Zurich, and New York. Despite the raging world economic crisis, where even the wealthy had to act shrewdly to keep whatever they had, the *Werkstätte* was able to open another branch in Berlin in 1929. However, not even this sweeping success could prevent the impending end of the *Werkstätte*.

Mismanagement and bad decisions paved the way for a declaration of bankruptcy in 1932.

Nevertheless, the legacy remains. The greatest international success of the *Werkstätte* was the *Jugendstil*-mansion of magnate Adolphe Stoclet, which was built according to blueprints from Josef Hoffmann in Brussels. Fernand Khnopff crafted the décor for the music room while Gustav Klimt decorated the dining room with his famous *Stoclet-Frieze*. Today, the *Palais Stoclet* is deservedly part of the list of UNESCO World Heritage sites.

Eduard Josef Wimmer-Wisgrill, ▶
Fabric sample *Ameise* (Ant), c. 1919. Raw silk, block printed, 22.5 x 30 cm.
Execution: *Wiener Werkstätte* (Vienna Workshop), no 33.
MAK - Österreichisches Museum für angewandte Kunst/ Gegenwartskunst, Vienna. Photograph by Nathan Murrell.

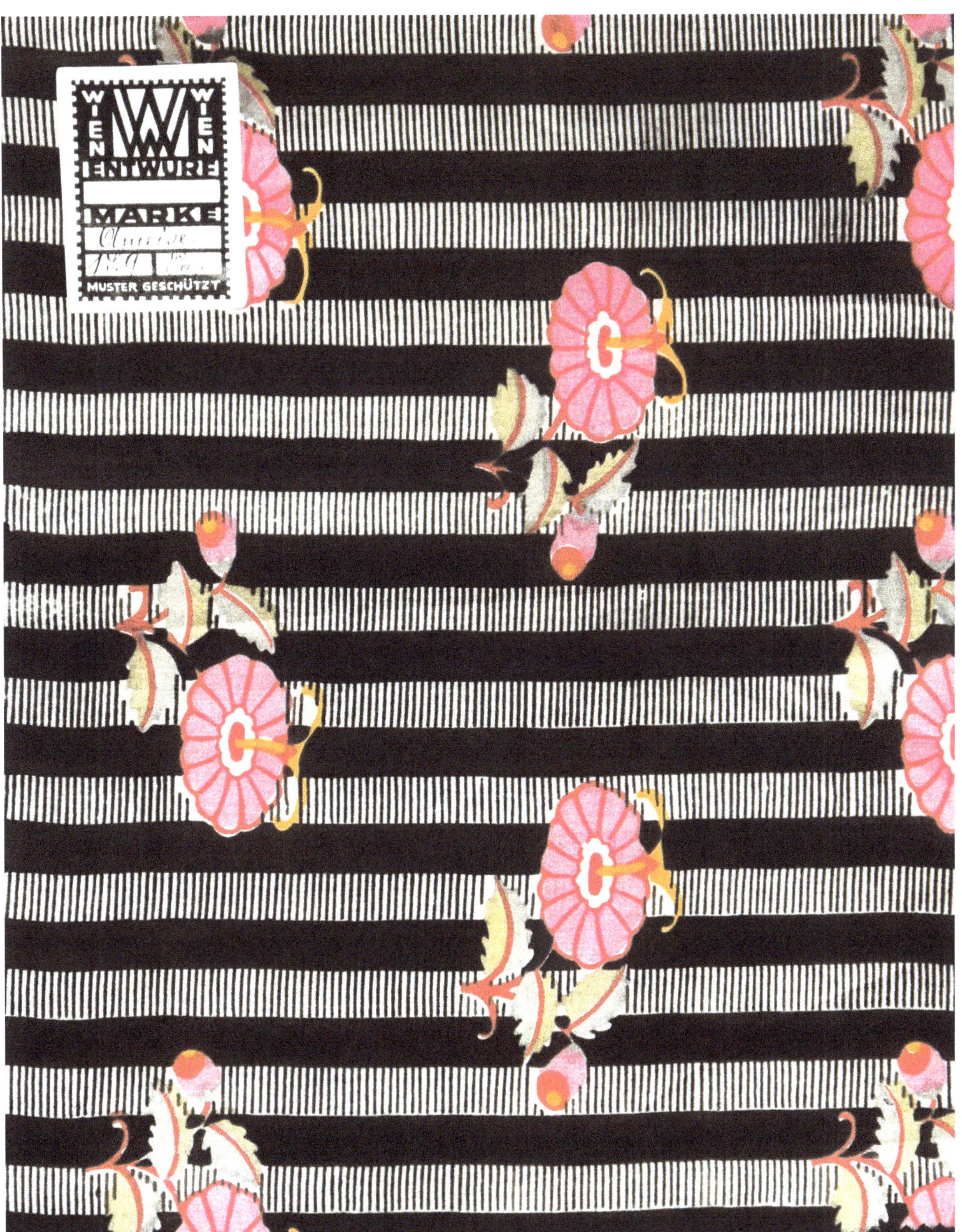

LIST OF ILLUSTRATIONS

ART HISTORY COLLECTION

Abstract Art	Naive Art
Art Deco	Neoclassicism
Art Nouveau	Persian Art
Baroque	Post-Impressionism
Byzantine Art	Realism
Chinese Art	Renaissance
Cubism	Pre-Raphaelites
Dada	Rococo
Early Italian Art	Roman Art
Egypt Art	Romanesque Art
Expressionism	Romanticism
Gothic Art	Surrealism
Greek Art	Symbolism
Impressionism	The Fauves
Indian Art	The Viennese Secession